The
PREPARATION

BY

DEBAABRATA DHARR

The

Preparation

Cornerstone of Achievements

By

Debaabrata Dharr

The book "Preparation" is dedicated to my sons Debapratim and Debajit and to all my students who are in the stage of preparation for higher achievements.

Acknowledgements

Writing "Preparation: Cornerstone of Achievement" has been a remarkable journey, and I am deeply grateful to everyone who has supported and inspired me along the way.

First and foremost, I would like to thank my family for their unwavering support and encouragement. Your belief in me has been a constant source of motivation, and your patience throughout this process has been invaluable.

To my friends and colleagues, thank you for your insights, feedback, and the countless discussions that have shaped this book. Your perspectives and experiences have enriched my understanding and added depth to my work.

I am also deeply grateful to my mentor, whose guidance and wisdom have been instrumental in shaping my thoughts and approach. Your support has been a cornerstone of my personal and professional growth.

A special thanks to my editor and publishing team for their dedication and expertise. Your meticulous attention to detail and commitment to excellence have brought this book to life.

Lastly, I would like to extend my gratitude to my readers. Your interest and enthusiasm for this subject have been a driving force behind this project. I hope this book serves as a valuable resource on your path to achievement.

Thank you all for being a part of this journey.

Sincerely,

Debaabrata Dharr

Declaration

I am thrilled to introduce my book, "Preparation: Cornerstone of Achievement," a comprehensive guide designed to empower individuals to harness the transformative power of preparation in their journey toward success. This book explores the fundamental role that meticulous planning, strategic foresight, and disciplined practice play in achieving our highest aspirations. Through a blend of insightful theories, practical advice, and inspiring anecdotes, "Preparation" aims to be your go-to resource for mastering the art of being ready—whatever your goals may be. Embrace this cornerstone and unlock your full potential for remarkable achievement.

An Open Letter to My Readers:

Unlocking Your Potential

Dear Readers,

Life is a journey brimming with untapped potential and endless possibilities. Each of you holds within yourself a powerhouse of talents, dreams, and abilities waiting to be unleashed. Often, we find ourselves doubting our capacities or hesitating to take the first step towards our aspirations. Today, I want to remind you of the incredible potential you possess and how with proper preparation, discipline, and consistency, you can achieve anything you set your mind to.

Preparation: Laying the Foundation

Preparation is the cornerstone of any great endeavor. Just as a builder plans meticulously before constructing a house, you must lay a solid foundation for your goals. This means acquiring the necessary knowledge, developing relevant skills, and understanding the path ahead. Whether you're aiming for a career milestone, personal growth, or a new venture, thorough preparation will set you up for success. Embrace the learning process, seek out resources, and never shy away from asking for guidance.

Discipline: The Bridge to Success

Discipline is the bridge that connects your goals to your accomplishments. It involves making choices that align with your objectives, even when it's difficult. Discipline requires consistency in effort and a commitment to your path, regardless of the obstacles. It's about waking up early to work on your dream, staying focused amidst distractions, and persevering even when results are not immediately visible. Remember, every small, disciplined action accumulates over time, bringing you closer to your desired outcome.

Consistency: The Key to Sustained Progress

Consistency is the secret ingredient that sustains progress. It's not enough to make a grand effort once; true success lies in the ability to maintain steady progress over time. Consistent actions, no matter how small, compound to create significant results. Whether it's dedicating an hour daily to your craft, practicing mindfulness regularly, or setting aside time each week to review and adjust your plans, consistency ensures that you stay on track and continually move forward.

Believe in Your Powerhouse

You are a powerhouse of potential. Every one of you has unique strengths and capabilities that can change your life and the world around you. Believe in your ability to achieve greatness. Embrace the challenges, learn from failures, and celebrate every victory, no matter how small. Your journey to success is a testament to your resilience and determination.

Life is a beautiful tapestry woven with opportunities and potential. By preparing diligently, exercising discipline, and maintaining consistency, you can unlock your full potential and achieve the success you desire. The power lies within you, and the world is waiting to witness the incredible impact you are destined to make.

Stay inspired, stay focused, and keep moving forward.

With unwavering belief in your potential,

Your 's

Debaabrata Dharr

Preparation is the deliberate process of getting ready for a specific task, goal, or event. It involves planning, gathering resources, acquiring skills, and organizing oneself to effectively tackle challenges. Preparation is crucial for achieving success because it enhances performance, minimizes risks, and increases confidence. By preparing thoroughly, individuals can anticipate obstacles and develop strategies to overcome them, thus increasing their chances of reaching their objectives. In essence, preparation lays the foundation for success by ensuring that one is equipped with the necessary tools and mindset to excel in their endeavors.

Introduction:

In the journey of life, success often seems like a distant summit, shimmering on the horizon, beckoning us to reach higher and strive harder. Yet, amidst the cacophony of aspirations and dreams, there lies a silent but formidable force that serves as the bedrock upon which success is built: preparation. Like a masterful conductor orchestrating a symphony, preparation directs our actions, hones our skills, and propels us towards our goals with unwavering determination.

But what exactly is preparation? It is more than just a mere checklist or a series of tasks to be completed. Preparation is a mindset, a way of life—a deliberate and purposeful endeavor to ready oneself for the challenges and opportunities that lie ahead. It is the art of meticulously crafting our path, sharpening our tools, and fortifying our resolve in anticipation of the trials and triumphs that await us.

The significance of preparation in achieving success cannot be overstated. It is the cornerstone upon which greatness is erected, the secret weapon that separates the extraordinary from the mediocre. Without proper preparation, even the most talented individuals may falter in the face of adversity, their potential left unrealized amidst the chaos of uncharted waters.

In this book, we embark on a journey to unravel the mysteries of preparation and explore its profound significance in the pursuit of success. Through illuminating insights, practical strategies, and inspiring anecdotes, we delve deep into the essence of preparation, uncovering its transformative power and timeless wisdom.

Join me as we navigate the labyrinth of preparation, unlocking its secrets and harnessing its boundless potential to propel us towards the summit of success. For in the realm of achievement, those who prepare with purpose and passion are destined to conquer the highest peaks and carve their legacy upon the annals of history.

Chapter 1: *The Power of Preparation*

Story

Mahendra Singh Dhoni, fondly known as MS Dhoni, rose from humble beginnings to become one of India's most celebrated cricketers. His journey to success was marked by meticulous preparation, unwavering determination, and a relentless pursuit of excellence.

From the dusty streets of Ranchi, Jharkhand, Dhoni's love for cricket burned bright. He honed his skills playing in local tournaments and matches, catching the eye of coaches and selectors with his natural talent and unconventional style of play.

But Dhoni knew that talent alone wouldn't be enough to make it to the top. He dedicated himself to rigorous training, spending countless hours in the nets perfecting his batting, wicket-keeping, and leadership skills.

Dhoni's preparation extended beyond the physical aspects of the game. He studied the strategies of top players and teams, analyzing their strengths and weaknesses to refine his own approach to the game. He also focused on mental preparation, cultivating a calm and composed demeanor under pressure.

His breakthrough came in 2004 when he made his debut for the Indian cricket team. Despite facing initial skepticism due to his unorthodox style, Dhoni quickly silenced his critics with his fearless batting and sharp wicket-keeping skills.

As his career progressed, Dhoni's leadership qualities shone through. In 2007, he was appointed captain of the Indian team for the inaugural ICC T20 World Cup. Against all odds, Dhoni led his team to victory, showcasing his ability to remain cool under pressure and make bold decisions in crunch situations.

Under Dhoni's captaincy, India reached new heights in international cricket, winning the ICC Cricket World Cup in 2011 and the ICC Champions Trophy in 2013. His astute leadership and tactical acumen earned him widespread admiration and respect, both on and off the field.

Throughout his career, Dhoni remained grounded and humble, never letting success go to his head. He continued to push himself to improve, constantly seeking new challenges and opportunities for growth.

In 2020, Dhoni announced his retirement from international cricket, leaving behind a legacy that will be remembered for generations to come. His journey from a small-town boy to a cricketing legend is a testament to the power of meticulous preparation, unwavering determination, and a relentless pursuit of excellence.

The Dragon's Discipline:

 Bruce Lee's Path to Martial Arts Mastery

In the swirling mist of Hong Kong's Kowloon district, a legend was born. Bruce Lee, the future icon of martial arts, entered the world on November 27, 1940. From his earliest days, Lee's life was infused with the spirit of discipline and dedication that would come to define him.

Growing up in post-war Hong Kong, Lee's childhood was marked by a mixture of privilege and adversity. His father, a famous Cantonese opera star, imbued him with a love for performance and athleticism. But it was his mother who instilled in him the values of hard work and determination.

From a young age, Lee showed a natural inclination towards martial arts. His first introduction came through the ancient art of Wing Chun, under the guidance of the legendary master, Ip Man. Under Ip Man's tutelage, Lee honed his skills with relentless dedication, spending hours each day practicing the intricate movements and techniques of the discipline.

But Lee's hunger for knowledge was insatiable. He voraciously studied other martial arts styles, including Taekwondo, Judo, and Boxing, seeking to synthesize the most effective techniques into his own unique system. His quest for mastery led him to the United States, where he would further refine his craft and leave an indelible mark on the world of martial arts.

Arriving in San Francisco in 1959, Lee faced a new set of challenges. As an Asian immigrant in America, he encountered prejudice and discrimination at every turn. But rather than succumbing to bitterness or despair, Lee used these obstacles as fuel for his ambition. He enrolled at the University of Washington, studying philosophy and psychology while continuing to train and teach martial arts.

Lee's reputation as a martial arts prodigy quickly spread throughout the Bay Area. Students flocked to his classes, drawn by his charisma and his innovative approach to combat. But behind the flashy exterior lay a man of unparalleled discipline and focus. Lee's training regimen was legendary, consisting of grueling workouts and relentless practice sessions that pushed his body and mind to their limits.

One of the cornerstones of Lee's philosophy was his belief in the importance of adaptability. He famously said, "Be like water, my friend. Empty your mind, be formless, shapeless, like water." This fluidity of thought and action became the hallmark of his martial arts style, known as Jeet Kune Do.

Lee's dedication to his craft was unwavering. He would spend hours analyzing footage of his fights, dissecting every movement and strategy to uncover ways to improve. He pushed himself to the brink of exhaustion, constantly seeking to push past his own limitations and unlock new levels of skill and understanding.

But Lee's journey was not without its setbacks. In 1964, he suffered a debilitating back injury that left him bedridden for six months. Doctors told him he would never be able to practice martial arts again. But Lee refused to accept defeat. Through sheer force of will and an unshakeable belief in his own abilities, he not only recovered from his injury but emerged stronger and more determined than ever before.

Lee's dedication to his craft eventually caught the attention of Hollywood. In 1971, he was cast in the role that would make him a household name: the enigmatic martial artist, Lee in the film "The Big Boss". His electrifying performance captivated audiences around the world and launched him to international superstardom.

But fame and fortune were never Lee's primary motivations. For him, martial arts were not just a means of self-expression, but a way of life. He saw it as a path to self-discovery and personal growth, a philosophy that he sought to share with the world through his writings and teachings.

Tragically, Bruce Lee's life was cut short on July 20, 1973, when he passed away at the age of 32. But his legacy lives on, a testament to the power of dedication, discipline, and the relentless pursuit of excellence. Today, Bruce Lee is remembered not just as a martial arts icon, but as a symbol of resilience and determination, inspiring countless individuals to follow in his footsteps and reach for greatness.

Part 2

Being prepared boosts confidence because it reduces uncertainty and increases a sense of control. Psychologically, preparation provides a sense of mastery and competence, leading to greater self-assurance. It also helps alleviate anxiety and stress, as individuals feel more capable of handling whatever challenges may arise. Additionally, preparedness allows people to focus more on their strengths and abilities rather than worrying about potential pitfalls, further enhancing their confidence levels.

Lights, Camera, Confidence: The Rise of Mr. Bean

In the heart of London's vibrant theater district, there lived a young man named Rowan. From a tender age, Rowan harbored a deep passion for the performing arts. His love for storytelling and making people laugh was evident in every impromptu skit he performed for family and friends.

Despite his natural talent, Rowan's journey to stardom was fraught with self-doubt and uncertainty. Growing up in a small town, he often felt like an outsider, struggling to find his place in the world. But deep down, he knew that his dreams were worth pursuing, no matter how daunting the obstacles seemed.

As Rowan entered adulthood, he made the bold decision to pursue acting as a career. Armed with nothing but his boundless enthusiasm and unwavering determination, he set out to conquer the cutthroat world of show business.

His first audition was a nerve-wracking experience. Surrounded by seasoned professionals, Rowan couldn't help but feel like a fish out of water. But instead of letting fear paralyze him, he channeled his nervous energy into preparing for the audition.

For weeks leading up to the big day, Rowan immersed himself in the role, studying the character's motivations, quirks, and mannerisms. He rehearsed tirelessly, fine-tuning every gesture and inflection until it felt just right. By the time he walked into the audition room, he was no longer just Rowan - he was the character, fully immersed in the world of the play.

Despite his best efforts, Rowan didn't land the role. But instead of being discouraged, he saw it as an opportunity to learn and grow. He sought feedback from the casting director, eager to improve and refine his craft. And with each rejection, he emerged stronger and more determined than ever before.

Rowan's perseverance soon caught the eye of a seasoned acting coach, who saw potential in the young performer. Under his guidance, Rowan honed his skills, learning the intricacies of stagecraft and the art of embodying a character. He immersed himself in the works of theater greats, drawing inspiration from their performances and techniques.

Armed with newfound knowledge and a renewed sense of purpose, Rowan set out to conquer the stage. Audition after audition, he poured his heart and soul into every performance, leaving a lasting impression on casting directors and audiences alike. And slowly but surely, his hard work began to pay off.

It wasn't long before Rowan landed his breakthrough role - a quirky, lovable character named Mr. Bean. With his signature tweed jacket, rubbery face, and childlike innocence, Mr. Bean captured the hearts of millions around the world. His antics and misadventures brought joy and laughter to audiences of all ages, cementing Rowan's status as a bona fide star.

But behind the scenes, Rowan's success was anything but overnight. It was the result of years of preparation, dedication, and unwavering belief in himself. Each episode of Mr. Bean was meticulously crafted, with Rowan pouring over every detail to ensure that it was nothing short of perfection.

As Mr. Bean's popularity soared, so too did Rowan's confidence. Gone were the days of self-doubt and insecurity - he stood tall, proud of the work he had accomplished and excited for the challenges that lay ahead. He embraced his unique brand of comedy, trusting in his instincts and staying true to himself no matter what.

Through his portrayal of Mr. Bean, Rowan inspired countless aspiring actors to embrace their quirks and celebrate their individuality. He showed them that success wasn't about conforming to society's standards, but about staying true to oneself and pursuing one's passions with unwavering confidence.

And so, as Rowan looked back on his journey from small-town dreamer to international sensation, he couldn't help but marvel at how far he had come. It was a testament to the power of preparation, perseverance, and believing in oneself - lessons he hoped to impart to future generations of performers for years to come.

Psychologically, preparation provides a sense of mastery and competence, leading to greater self-assurance.

The Journey of a Legend: Michael Jordan's Path to Greatness

In the heart of Wilmington, North Carolina, a young boy named Michael Jordan dreamt of soaring through the air like his basketball heroes. From a humble beginning, he honed his skills on the court, fueled by a burning desire to excel.

As a high school standout, Jordan faced early setbacks, failing to make the varsity team in his sophomore year. But instead of succumbing to defeat, he turned it into motivation, training tirelessly to prove himself. With each dribble, each shot, he cultivated not just physical prowess, but mental resilience.

His journey continued at the University of North Carolina, where he showcased his talent and tenacity, winning a national championship and earning accolades as College Player of the Year. But Jordan's hunger for greatness was insatiable.

In 1984, he entered the NBA draft, joining the Chicago Bulls as the third overall pick. From the moment he stepped onto the professional stage, Jordan captivated audiences with his electrifying play. His aerial acrobatics and killer instinct made him a force to be reckoned with.

However, it wasn't just his athleticism that propelled him to superstardom; it was his unwavering dedication to preparation. Jordan famously said, "I've failed over and over and over again in my life. And that is why I succeed." Each failure only fueled his determination to work harder, to push himself beyond his limits.

With each passing season, Jordan's legend grew. He led the Bulls to six NBA championships, earning five MVP awards along the way. His list of accomplishments seemed endless: scoring titles, All-Star selections, Olympic gold medals. But behind the highlights and headlines was a man who understood the power of preparation.

Whether it was his rigorous training regimen, his meticulous study of opponents, or his relentless pursuit of perfection, Jordan approached every game with a sense of mastery and competence. And it was this self-assurance that set him apart from his peers.

Off the court, Jordan's influence extended far beyond basketball. His relentless work ethic and competitive spirit inspired millions around the globe. He became a cultural icon, synonymous with excellence and determination.

Today, Michael Jordan's legacy endures as a testament to the power of preparation and perseverance. His journey from a small-town kid to a global icon serves as a reminder that greatness is not bestowed upon the chosen few, but earned through hard work, dedication, and an unwavering belief in oneself.

One incident that exemplifies Michael Jordan's psychological preparation before games is the "Flu Game" during the 1997 NBA Finals. In Game 5 against the Utah Jazz, Jordan was suffering from flu-like symptoms, including nausea and fever. Despite his illness, Jordan decided to play.

Before the game, Jordan's mental fortitude was on full display. Despite feeling weak and sick, he focused his mind on the task at hand, blocking out distractions and doubts. His determination to compete at the highest level drove him to push through the adversity.

During the game, Jordan's preparation and mental toughness shone through as he delivered one of the most memorable performances of his career. Despite his physical condition, he scored 38 points, leading the Chicago Bulls to a crucial victory. His ability to maintain his focus and elevate his performance despite adversity showcased his unparalleled psychological preparation before games.

Preparedness allows people to focus more on their strengths and abilities rather than worrying about potential pitfalls, further enhancing their confidence levels.

The Power of Preparedness:

Arunima Sinha's Triumph on Mt. Everest

Preparedness is a powerful tool that enables individuals to channel their focus towards their strengths and abilities, rather than being consumed by worries about potential obstacles. This focus, in turn, enhances confidence levels, allowing individuals to overcome even the most daunting challenges. Arunima Sinha's remarkable journey of conquering Mount Everest despite her physical challenges exemplifies the transformative impact of preparedness on confidence and achievement.

Preparedness acts as a mental anchor, directing attention away from apprehensions and towards one's strengths and capabilities. By meticulously planning and training, individuals like Arunima Sinha can develop a sense of control over their circumstances, allowing them to navigate challenges with confidence. In Sinha's case, her rigorous physical training and mental preparation helped her shift her focus from the daunting prospect of climbing Everest with a prosthetic leg to the belief in her own resilience and determination.

Preparedness magnifies individuals' strengths, enabling them to leverage their abilities to their fullest potential. Arunima Sinha's unwavering determination, resilience, and indomitable spirit were fortified through months of intense preparation and training. Her physical strength, mental fortitude, and mountaineering skills were honed to perfection, allowing her to approach the Everest expedition with unwavering confidence.

Preparedness equips individuals with the tools and strategies necessary to overcome potential pitfalls and adversities. For Arunima Sinha, the journey to Mount Everest was fraught with numerous challenges, including the physical demands of high-altitude climbing and the inherent risks associated with her prosthetic leg. However, her thorough preparation, coupled with a positive mindset, enabled her to navigate these obstacles with grace and resilience.

Preparedness breeds confidence, serving as the catalyst for success in the face of adversity. Arunima Sinha's unshakeable self-belief and confidence in her abilities were instrumental in her historic ascent of Mount Everest. Despite the doubts and naysayers, Sinha remained steadfast in her conviction, drawing strength from her preparation and unwavering determination to prove her critics wrong.

Arunima Sinha's conquest of Mount Everest stands as a testament to the transformative power of preparedness. Despite losing her leg in a tragic accident, Sinha refused to let adversity define her. Instead, she embraced her physical challenges as an opportunity to inspire others and prove the limitless potential of the human spirit. Through meticulous planning, rigorous training, and unwavering determination, Sinha not only scaled the world's highest peak but also shattered stereotypes and redefined the boundaries of what is possible.

The story of Arunima Sinha's triumph on Mount Everest underscores the profound impact of preparedness on confidence and achievement. By focusing on her strengths and abilities, Sinha was able to overcome daunting challenges and achieve the seemingly impossible. Her journey serves as a powerful reminder that with thorough preparation, unwavering determination, and a positive mindset, individuals can conquer any obstacle and achieve their dreams.

Assessing goals and objectives to determine the necessary preparations.

To assess goals and objectives effectively, consider these steps:

Define Clear Goals: Understand the desired outcome or result.

Break Down Goals: Divide big goals into smaller, manageable objectives.

Identify Resources: Determine what resources are needed to achieve each objective.

Evaluate Skills: Assess the skills and competencies required for success.

Plan Preparations: Develop a detailed plan outlining the necessary steps and preparations.

Allocate Time: Set realistic timelines for completing each preparation.

Monitor Progress: Regularly review progress and make adjustments as needed.

Stay Flexible: Be open to adapting plans based on changing circumstances or new information.

By following these steps, you can effectively prepare to achieve your goals and objectives.

Defining clear goals involves understanding the desired outcome or result you want to achieve. Here's how to do it effectively:

Be Specific: Clearly define what you want to accomplish. Avoid vague statements and instead, use precise language.

Make it Measurable: Establish criteria for measuring progress toward your goal. Quantifiable metrics help track your success.

Ensure Relevance: Align your goals with your broader objectives and priorities. They should contribute meaningfully to your overall mission or vision.

Set Achievable Targets: Make sure your goals are realistic and attainable within the given constraints, such as time, resources, and capabilities.

Define Timeframes: Establish a timeline for achieving your goals. Setting deadlines creates a sense of urgency and helps you stay focused.

Consider Potential Challenges: Anticipate obstacles or barriers that may arise and plan accordingly. Having contingency plans can keep you on track when faced with setbacks.

Seek Clarity: Communicate your goals clearly to stakeholders involved, ensuring everyone understands the desired outcome and their role in achieving it.

By following these steps, you can define clear and actionable goals that guide your efforts effectively.

Tenzing Norgay: Conquering Everest's Summit

High in the majestic Himalayas, where the air thins and the mountains reach for the heavens, lived a man whose name would become synonymous with triumph and perseverance: Tenzing Norgay.

Born into a humble Sherpa family in the Khumbu region of Nepal, Tenzing was destined for greatness from a young age. As a child, he roamed the rugged terrain surrounding his village, learning the ways of the mountains from his elders. His curiosity and resilience knew no bounds, and he dreamed of scaling the highest peaks, despite the dangers that lurked in their icy depths.

Tenzing's journey to the top of the world began long before he ever set foot on Mount Everest. His early years were marked by hardship and adversity, yet he faced each challenge with unwavering determination. From a young age, he worked as a porter, carrying loads for expeditions venturing into the Himalayas. It was grueling work, but Tenzing's strength and endurance set him apart from his peers.

As he honed his skills in the mountains, Tenzing caught the eye of seasoned climbers who recognized his innate talent and drive. Among them was the legendary explorer Sir Edmund Hillary, whose name would become forever intertwined with Tenzing's in the annals of mountaineering history.

Their paths first crossed in 1951, when Hillary joined a reconnaissance expedition to Everest's southern face. Impressed by Tenzing's expertise and mountain prowess, Hillary knew he had found a kindred spirit in the Sherpa climber. The two formed a bond that would withstand the most formidable challenges nature could muster.

It was not until three years later, in 1953, that Tenzing and Hillary embarked on their historic attempt to conquer Everest's summit. Armed with determination, courage, and a shared vision of reaching the pinnacle of human achievement, they set out from base camp, each step bringing them closer to their ultimate goal.

The journey was fraught with peril at every turn. They battled fierce winds, treacherous crevasses, and bone-chilling cold as they ascended into the unforgiving realm of the "Death Zone," where the air is so thin that even the slightest misstep could prove fatal.

But Tenzing and Hillary pressed on, fueled by a combination of sheer willpower and the unshakable belief that they were destined to succeed. Their bond grew stronger with each passing day, as they relied on each other for support and encouragement in the face of overwhelming odds.

Finally, on the morning of May 29, 1953, Tenzing and Hillary stood at the summit of Mount Everest, the highest point on Earth. In that moment of triumph, they defied the limits of human endurance and proved that anything is possible with courage, perseverance, and a steadfast determination to succeed.

Their achievement reverberated around the world, inspiring countless others to reach for their own Everest, whatever form it may take. But for Tenzing Norgay, the journey was far from over. In the years that followed, he continued to push the boundaries of exploration, becoming a beacon of hope and inspiration for future generations of adventurers.

Today, Tenzing's legacy lives on in the hearts of all who dare to dream big and strive for greatness. His story serves as a testament to the power of the human spirit and the enduring allure of the world's highest peaks. And though he may have left this world behind, his indomitable spirit continues to soar among the clouds, forever etched into the fabric of mountaineering history.

Breaking down big goals into smaller, manageable objectives can help make them more achievable. Here's a step-by-step strategy to do that:

Define Your Big Goal: Start by clearly defining your overarching goal. Make sure it's specific, measurable, achievable, relevant, and time-bound (SMART).

Identify Major Milestones: Break down your big goal into major milestones or key stages that you need to accomplish to achieve the overall objective.

Brainstorm Smaller Objectives: For each milestone, brainstorm smaller objectives or tasks that need to be completed to reach that milestone. These should be specific and actionable.

Prioritize Tasks: Determine which tasks are most critical or time-sensitive. Prioritize them accordingly to ensure you're focusing on the right things at the right time.

Set Deadlines: Assign deadlines to each smaller objective to keep yourself accountable and ensure progress is being made consistently.

Allocate Resources: Identify the resources you'll need to accomplish each task, whether it's time, money, people, or tools, and allocate them accordingly.

Create an Action Plan: Develop a detailed action plan outlining the specific steps you'll take to achieve each smaller objective. Break it down into daily, weekly, or monthly tasks as needed.

Monitor Progress: Regularly track your progress against the smaller objectives and milestones. This will help you stay on track and make adjustments if necessary.

Celebrate Achievements: Acknowledge and celebrate each milestone and smaller objective you accomplish along the way. This will help keep you motivated and energized.

Review and Adjust: Periodically review your progress and reassess your strategies. Make adjustments as needed based on what's working well and what isn't.

By following these steps, you can effectively break down your big goals into smaller, manageable objectives and create a clear roadmap for success.

Crafting a Clear Vision and Roadmap for Success

A clear vision and roadmap are essential elements for achieving success in any endeavor. They provide direction, clarity, and purpose, guiding individuals and organizations toward their goals.

Why Vision Matters:

Provides Clarity: A well-defined vision clarifies the purpose and goals of an individual or organization, ensuring everyone understands what they are working towards.

Inspires Motivation: A compelling vision inspires people to work towards a common goal, motivating them to overcome obstacles and persevere in the face of challenges.

Aligns Efforts: A shared vision aligns the efforts of team members or stakeholders, fostering collaboration and synergy towards a common objective.

Components of a Clear Vision:

Mission Statement: Clearly articulate the purpose and values that drive your actions.

Long-Term Goals: Define specific, measurable objectives that reflect your vision for the future.

Core Values: Identify the guiding principles that inform decision-making and behavior.

Vivid Description: Paint a vivid picture of what success looks like, creating a compelling image that resonates with stakeholders.

Creating a Roadmap for Success:

Assess Current Position: Evaluate strengths, weaknesses, opportunities, and threats to determine where you stand.

Set SMART Goals: Develop specific, measurable, achievable, relevant, and time-bound goals that support your vision.

Prioritize Actions: Identify key initiatives and prioritize them based on their impact and feasibility.

Allocate Resources: Determine the resources required to execute your roadmap effectively, including finances, personnel, and time.

Establish Milestones: Break down goals into smaller, manageable tasks and set milestones to track progress.

Monitor and Adjust: Continuously monitor progress, evaluate results, and make adjustments as needed to stay on course.

Tips for Implementation:

Communicate Effectively: Ensure everyone understands the vision, roadmap, and their role in achieving success.

Foster Accountability: Hold individuals and teams accountable for their contributions and outcomes.

Embrace Flexibility: Be open to changes and adaptations as circumstances evolve, while staying true to your overarching vision.

Celebrate Achievements: Recognize and celebrate milestones and successes along the journey, reinforcing commitment and motivation.

Case Studies:

SpaceX: Elon Musk's vision of making humanity a multi-planetary species has guided SpaceX's efforts to revolutionize space exploration.

Google: Google's mission to organize the world's information and make it universally accessible and useful has driven its innovation and expansion into various industries.

Case Study: Apple Inc.

Apple Inc. stands as a quintessential example of how a clear vision and roadmap for success can transform a company from near obscurity to global dominance. Founded by Steve Jobs, Steve Wozniak, and Ronald Wayne in 1976, Apple began its journey in a small garage with a vision to revolutionize the personal computing industry. Let's delve into how Apple developed and executed its vision and roadmap for success:

Vision Formation:

Apple's vision was clear from the outset: to democratize computing and empower individuals through user-friendly technology. Steve Jobs envisioned a future where technology seamlessly integrated into people's lives, enhancing creativity, productivity, and communication.

Mission Statement:

Apple's mission statement evolved over time but remained centered on innovation and customer-centricity. Jobs famously stated, "We're here to put a dent in the universe," encapsulating Apple's ambition to push boundaries and challenge the status quo.

Long-Term Goals:

Apple's long-term goals were ambitious yet focused. From launching the groundbreaking Macintosh in 1984 to revolutionizing the music industry with the iPod in 2001, each product release was strategically aligned with the overarching vision of simplicity and elegance in design.

Core Values:

Apple's core values, including innovation, design excellence, and customer experience, permeated every aspect of the company's culture and operations. Jobs instilled a relentless pursuit of perfection and attention to detail, fostering a culture of excellence and creativity.

Vivid Description:

Jobs had a knack for painting vivid pictures of Apple's future. His iconic product launches, characterized by minimalist aesthetics and captivating presentations, captured the imagination of audiences worldwide and reinforced Apple's vision of a connected, digital lifestyle.

Roadmap for Success:

Product Development:

Apple's roadmap for success revolved around continuous innovation and product differentiation. The company invested heavily in research and development, pushing the boundaries of technology to deliver groundbreaking products that set industry standards.

Market Expansion:

Apple strategically expanded its market reach, transitioning from personal computers to consumer electronics, software services, and digital content distribution. The introduction of the iPhone in 2007 marked a pivotal moment, propelling Apple into the mobile industry and redefining the smartphone market.

Ecosystem Integration:

Apple focused on building an ecosystem of seamlessly integrated products and services, fostering customer loyalty and lock-in. The synergy between hardware, software, and services, exemplified by the Apple ecosystem, created a unique value proposition for consumers.

Brand Building:

Apple's brand strategy emphasized emotional appeal and aspirational lifestyle marketing. The company cultivated a strong brand identity characterized by simplicity, sophistication, and innovation, resonating with consumers across demographics and geographies.

Sustainability and Social Responsibility:

In recent years, Apple has incorporated sustainability and social responsibility into its roadmap for success. From renewable energy initiatives to supply chain transparency and labor rights advocacy, Apple has demonstrated a commitment to making a positive impact on society and the environment.

Apple's journey from humble beginnings to global prominence exemplifies the power of a clear vision and roadmap for success. By staying true to its core values, relentlessly pursuing innovation, and adapting to changing market dynamics, Apple has continued to thrive and shape the future of technology. The company's success story serves as inspiration for aspiring entrepreneurs and businesses seeking to chart their own path to success.

Developing a clear vision and roadmap for success is a foundational step towards achieving your goals. By defining your purpose, setting ambitious yet achievable goals, and outlining a strategic plan for execution, you can navigate the complexities of your journey with confidence and clarity. Stay focused, stay adaptable, and never lose sight of the vision that drives you forward.

Overcoming Challenges in Project Preparation

In any project, preparation is paramount. Yet, even the most meticulously planned projects can encounter unforeseen obstacles and challenges. In this case study, we delve into the journey of a fictional company, TechSolutions, as they navigate the preparation stage of a groundbreaking new product launch. Along the way, we identify potential obstacles and challenges and explore the strategies they employ to overcome them.

Case Study:

TechSolutions, a leading tech company, is on the verge of launching a revolutionary product that promises to disrupt the market. As they gear up for the launch, the preparation stage presents several potential obstacles and challenges.

Market Research and Analysis:

Obstacle: Limited understanding of the target market and consumer needs.

Strategy: TechSolutions conducts extensive market research, leveraging both quantitative data and qualitative insights. They employ surveys, focus groups, and competitor analysis to gain a comprehensive understanding of market dynamics and consumer preferences.

Resource Allocation:

Obstacle: Limited budget and resource constraints.

Strategy: TechSolutions adopts a strategic approach to resource allocation, prioritizing key areas such as product development, marketing, and customer support. They explore creative financing options, including partnerships and investor funding, to maximize their resources.

Technology and Infrastructure:

Obstacle: Technical challenges in product development and infrastructure setup.

Strategy: TechSolutions invests in cutting-edge technology and infrastructure, partnering with industry leaders to overcome technical hurdles. They prioritize scalability and reliability, ensuring their systems can handle the anticipated demand.

Regulatory Compliance:

Obstacle: Complex regulatory requirements and compliance issues.

Strategy: TechSolutions collaborates with legal experts to navigate the regulatory landscape effectively. They conduct thorough compliance audits and implement robust policies and procedures to ensure adherence to applicable laws and regulations.

Team Dynamics:

Obstacle: Potential conflicts and communication barriers within the project team.

Strategy: TechSolutions fosters a culture of open communication and collaboration, encouraging team members to voice their concerns and ideas. They invest in team-building activities and leadership development to enhance cohesion and synergy within the team.

Timeline and Deadlines:

Obstacle: Pressure to meet tight deadlines and project milestones.

Strategy: TechSolutions adopts a proactive approach to project management, utilizing tools such as Gantt charts and agile methodologies to track progress and identify potential bottlenecks. They prioritize tasks based on urgency and criticality, adjusting timelines as needed to ensure timely delivery.

External Dependencies:

Obstacle: Reliance on external vendors, partners, and suppliers.

Strategy: TechSolutions establishes strong partnerships and contingency plans to mitigate risks associated with external dependencies. They maintain open lines of communication with vendors and suppliers, setting clear expectations and monitoring performance closely.

In the face of numerous obstacles and challenges, TechSolutions successfully navigates the preparation stage of their project launch. Through strategic planning, effective communication, and a commitment to innovation, they overcome barriers and position themselves for success in the competitive marketplace. This case study underscores the importance of identifying potential obstacles early on and devising strategies to address them proactively, ensuring smooth project execution and delivery.

Chapter 3:

Planning for Success

Planning for success is crucial in the preparation stage across all fields because it helps set clear goals, identify potential obstacles, and establish strategies to overcome them. Whether in sports, business, or career, a well-thought-out plan provides direction, motivation, and a roadmap for achieving desired outcomes. It enables individuals and teams to maximize their resources, optimize their efforts, and adapt to changing circumstances effectively. In essence, planning lays the foundation for success by ensuring that efforts are focused, organized, and purposeful.

The art of strategic planning involves developing a comprehensive approach to achieving long-term goals by assessing internal and external factors, setting priorities, and allocating resources effectively. It works by aligning organizational objectives with actionable strategies, enabling proactive decision-making and adaptation to changes in the environment.

Strategic planning is highly beneficial as it provides clarity of purpose, enhances coordination and collaboration, and facilitates resource optimization. It also fosters innovation and growth by identifying opportunities and addressing challenges proactively.

A case study illustrating the effectiveness of strategic planning is the turnaround of Starbucks in the early 2000s. Facing declining sales and increased competition, Starbucks embarked on a strategic planning process to revitalize its brand and regain market share. The company focused on enhancing customer experience, expanding its product offerings, and improving operational efficiency. Through targeted initiatives such as store renovations, menu innovations, and employee training programs, Starbucks successfully repositioned itself as a premium coffee destination and achieved significant growth in sales and profitability.

By leveraging strategic planning principles, Starbucks was able to overcome challenges, capitalize on opportunities, and emerge stronger in the highly competitive coffee industry. This case demonstrates the transformative power of strategic planning in driving organizational success and sustainability.

Utilizing tools

In the journey of personal development, organization is key. Whether you're striving for career advancement, improving your health and wellness, or mastering a new skill, effective planning and organization can make all the difference.

Three powerful tools — timelines, checklists, and mind maps — and how you can harness their potential to organize your preparations effectively and achieve your goals.

Creating timelines, checklists, and mind maps for personal development can be highly effective for staying organized and focused. Here's how you can create each.

Section 1: Timelines

Timelines provide a visual representation of tasks and milestones over time, allowing you to track progress and stay on schedule. Here's how to create and utilize timelines for personal development:

Timelines:

* Start by identifying your ultimate goal or objective for personal development.

* Break down the goal into smaller, achievable milestones or tasks.

* Assign each milestone or task a deadline or estimated completion date.

* Use tools like Microsoft Excel, Google Sheets, or project management software to create your timeline. You can also use specialized timeline creation tools or even draw it by hand.

Section 2: Checklists

Checklists are simple yet powerful tools for organizing tasks and ensuring nothing falls through the cracks. Here's how to create and utilize checklists for personal development:

Checklists:

*Begin by listing all the tasks or activities you need to complete for your personal development.

*Break down larger tasks into smaller, actionable steps.

*Prioritize the tasks based on urgency or importance.

Create your checklist using digital tools like note-taking apps (e.g., Evernote, OneNote), task management apps (e.g., Todoist, Trello), or simply pen and paper.

Section 3: Mind Maps

Mind maps are versatile tools for visualizing ideas, connections, and plans. Here's how to create and utilize mind maps for personal development:

Mind Maps:

* Start with a central idea, which could be your main goal or theme for personal development.

* Branch out from the central idea by adding subtopics or categories related to your goal.

* Further expand each subtopic by adding specific tasks, strategies, or resources.

* Use mind mapping software like MindMeister, XMind, or even freehand drawing on paper or a whiteboard.

Remember to regularly review and update your timelines, checklists, and mind maps as you progress in your personal development journey. They should serve as dynamic tools to guide and track your growth effectively.

Timelines, checklists, and mind maps are invaluable tools for organizing preparations effectively and achieving personal development goals. By harnessing the power of these tools, you can clarify your objectives, track your progress, and stay motivated on your journey towards self-improvement. Remember to adapt these tools to suit your preferences and needs, and don't hesitate to experiment with different approaches until you find what works best for you. With dedication and strategic planning, you can unlock your full potential and reach new heights in your personal and professional life.

Allocating resources wisely for the preparation stage involves several key steps:

* **Assess Needs:** Identify what resources are required for the preparation stage, such as materials, equipment, personnel, and time.

* **Prioritize:** Determine which resources are most crucial and allocate them accordingly. Focus on essentials first before allocating resources to less critical aspects.

* **Budgeting:** Set a budget for the preparation stage to ensure resources are used efficiently. Consider factors like cost, availability, and quality when budgeting.

* **Efficiency:** Look for ways to maximize the efficiency of resource use, such as streamlining processes, reducing waste, and optimizing workflows.

* **Flexibility:** Be prepared to adapt resource allocation as needed based on changing circumstances or unexpected challenges during the preparation stage.

* **Monitoring and Adjusting:** Regularly monitor resource usage and adjust allocation as necessary to ensure that resources are being utilized effectively and in line with project goals.

* **Communication:** Maintain open communication with team members and stakeholders to ensure everyone is aware of resource allocation decisions and can provide input or feedback if needed.

By following these steps, you can allocate resources wisely to support the preparation stage effectively.

Here's a step-by-step process for allocating resources wisely to support the preparation process for career development:

* **Assessment of Career Goals:** Begin by assessing your career goals, including short-term and long-term objectives. Determine the skills, knowledge, and experiences needed to achieve these goals.

* **Identify Required Resources:** Based on your career goals, identify the resources necessary for preparation. This may include educational courses, workshops, certifications, mentorship programs, networking opportunities, books, online resources, and time for self-study.

* **Prioritize Resources:** Prioritize the identified resources based on their relevance to your career goals and their potential impact on your development. Focus on resources that align closely with your objectives and have the greatest potential to enhance your skills and knowledge.

* **Create a Resource Plan:** Develop a resource plan outlining how you will allocate your resources over time. Consider factors such as availability, cost, and time commitment when scheduling resource allocation.

* **Set a Budget:** Determine a budget for allocating resources to support your career development preparation. Allocate funds to different resources based on their importance and potential return on investment.

* **Research and Evaluate:** Research the available resources thoroughly to ensure they meet your needs and standards. Evaluate the quality, reputation, and effectiveness of each resource before making decisions.

* **Seek Support and Guidance:** Don't hesitate to seek support and guidance from mentors, career counselors, or industry professionals when allocating resources for career development. They can provide valuable insights and recommendations based on their experience.

* **Allocate Time Wisely:** Allocate time for career development activities in your schedule and commit to them consistently. Balance your time between different resources to ensure comprehensive preparation.

* **Monitor Progress:** Regularly monitor your progress in utilizing allocated resources for career development. Assess the effectiveness of each resource and adjust your resource allocation plan as needed based on your evolving needs and priorities.

* **Reflect and Adjust:** Reflect on your experiences and outcomes from using allocated resources. Identify areas for improvement and adjust your resource allocation strategy accordingly to optimize your career development preparation.

The Path to Success:

A Tale of Resource Allocation for Civil Services Exam Preparation

Once upon a time, in a bustling city, there lived a young aspiring civil servant named Maya. With a fervent desire to serve her country and make a difference in society, Maya embarked on a journey to prepare for the prestigious civil services exam.

As Maya delved into the daunting task of preparation, she realized the importance of allocating her resources wisely. With determination and a strategic mindset, she crafted a plan to make the most of her time, energy, and resources.

Firstly, Maya assessed her strengths and weaknesses, identifying the areas she needed to focus on for the exam. She recognized that comprehensive study materials, guidance from experts, and ample practice were essential resources for her preparation journey.

Maya prioritized her resources, allocating a significant portion of her time to self-study using high-quality textbooks, online courses, and educational resources. She meticulously planned her study schedule, dedicating specific hours each day to cover the vast syllabus comprehensively.

Understanding the value of mentorship, Maya sought guidance from experienced civil servants and academic professionals. She attended coaching classes and engaged in discussions with mentors to gain valuable insights and strategies for exam preparation.

To ensure she stayed motivated and on track, Maya surrounded herself with a supportive network of family and friends who encouraged her every step of the way. Their unwavering support served as a vital resource, bolstering her confidence and resolve during challenging times.

As Maya progressed in her preparation journey, she remained mindful of her budget constraints. She researched affordable yet effective study materials and coaching programs, making informed decisions to optimize her resource allocation without compromising on quality.

With perseverance and discipline, Maya diligently utilized her allocated resources, embracing every opportunity for growth and learning. She embraced mock tests and practice exams as valuable tools for self-assessment and improvement, refining her exam-taking skills and boosting her confidence.

As the day of the civil services exam drew near, Maya reflected on her journey of resource allocation. Through careful planning, prioritization, and perseverance, she had maximized her resources to support her preparation effectively.

On the day of the exam, Maya entered the examination hall with a sense of confidence and determination. Armed with the knowledge and skills acquired through her wise resource allocation, she tackled each question with precision and clarity.

Months later, as the results of the civil services exam were announced, Maya's heart raced with anticipation. To her joy and pride, she saw her name listed among the successful candidates. Maya's journey of resource allocation had culminated in a triumphant victory, opening doors to a future dedicated to serving her nation with passion and integrity.

In the end, Maya's story stood as a testament to the power of allocating resources wisely in pursuit of one's dreams. Through strategic planning, perseverance, and a steadfast commitment to excellence, she had paved her path to success in the civil services exam and beyond.

Chapter 4:

Cultivating Discipline and Consistency

The Crucial Role of Discipline in the Preparation Stage of Life's Journey

Life is a journey filled with various stages, each presenting its unique challenges and opportunities. Among these stages, the preparation stage stands out as a critical phase where discipline plays a paramount role. It is during this phase that individuals lay the foundation for their future endeavors, shaping their character, skills, and mindset for the challenges ahead.

Why Discipline Matters:

The preparation stage sets the tone for the rest of one's journey. Discipline acts as the guiding force that ensures individuals stay focused on their goals and aspirations, even when faced with distractions or setbacks.

This stage is where habits are formed, and discipline is the key to cultivating positive behaviors that contribute to personal growth and success. Whether it's practicing a skill daily or maintaining a healthy lifestyle, discipline ingrains habits that can last a lifetime.

Life's journey is bound to have its share of obstacles and disappointments. Discipline serves as the backbone of resilience, empowering individuals to persevere through tough times, learn from failures, and bounce back stronger.

Effective time management is crucial during the preparation stage, as it allows individuals to allocate their resources wisely and make the most out of their opportunities. Discipline helps in prioritizing tasks, avoiding procrastination, and staying focused on what truly matters.

Without discipline, goals remain mere wishes. Discipline transforms aspirations into actionable plans and ensures consistent effort towards their realization. It instills the dedication and perseverance needed to overcome challenges and reach new heights.

Practical Strategies for Cultivating Discipline:

Set Clear Goals: Define specific, achievable goals that align with your long-term vision. Break them down into smaller tasks and create a plan to tackle them systematically.

Establish Routines: Develop daily routines and stick to them religiously. Whether it's waking up early, exercising regularly, or dedicating time to study or work, routines reinforce discipline and promote consistency.

Stay Accountable: Share your goals with trusted friends, family members, or mentors who can hold you accountable for your actions. Regular check-ins and progress updates can help stay on track and motivated.

Practice Self-Control: Learn to resist temptations and distractions that derail your progress. Practice delayed gratification and focus on long-term rewards rather than immediate satisfaction.

Embrace Failure: Understand that setbacks are inevitable on the journey to success. Instead of letting failure deter you, use it as an opportunity to learn, grow, and refine your approach.

The preparation stage of life's journey lays the groundwork for future achievements and experiences. Discipline serves as the cornerstone of this phase, empowering individuals to stay focused, resilient, and committed to their goals. By cultivating discipline early on, individuals set themselves up for success and pave the way for a fulfilling and rewarding journey ahead.

The Art of Consistency and Motivation: *Navigating the Preparation Journey*

Embarking on a journey of preparation, whether it's for an exam, a project, or a personal goal, is often exhilarating at the outset. However, as time progresses, maintaining consistency and motivation can become challenging. This journey requires dedication, perseverance, and a strategic approach to stay on track amidst obstacles and distractions. In this discourse, we delve into the dynamics of consistency and motivation, exploring strategies to sustain them throughout the preparation journey.

Understanding Consistency:

Consistency is the cornerstone of progress. It involves the steadfast adherence to a set of actions, habits, or routines over time. Consistency fosters discipline, builds momentum, and cultivates a sense of reliability. To maintain consistency, it's crucial to establish clear goals, create a structured plan, and prioritize tasks effectively. Breaking down larger objectives into smaller, manageable tasks can make the journey less daunting and more achievable. Additionally, holding oneself accountable through tracking progress and celebrating milestones along the way reinforces consistency.

Cultivating Motivation:

Motivation is the driving force behind action. It fuels ambition, sustains effort, and propels individuals towards their aspirations. However, motivation is not always constant; it fluctuates based on various factors such as external influences, internal mindset, and emotional state. To cultivate motivation, it's essential to align goals with personal values and aspirations, fostering a sense of purpose and meaning in the journey. Setting realistic expectations, visualizing success, and surrounding oneself with a supportive environment can also enhance motivation. Moreover, practicing self-care, managing stress, and finding inspiration in setbacks and challenges can reignite motivation during difficult times.

Strategies for Sustaining Consistency and Motivation:

Establish a Routine: Consistency thrives in structure. Design a daily or weekly routine that allocates dedicated time for preparation activities. Consistency becomes habitual when integrated into one's lifestyle.

Set SMART Goals: Specific, Measurable, Achievable, Relevant, and Time-bound goals provide clarity and direction. Break down long-term goals into smaller milestones, making progress tangible and attainable.

Prioritize Tasks: Identify high-priority tasks and allocate time and resources accordingly. Focus on activities that align with long-term objectives, avoiding distractions and procrastination.

Find Meaning and Purpose: Connect preparation efforts to personal values and long-term aspirations. Understanding the significance of the journey enhances motivation and perseverance.

Cultivate a Growth Mindset: Embrace challenges, view failures as learning opportunities, and believe in the capacity for growth and improvement. A growth mindset fosters resilience and tenacity in the face of adversity.

Seek Support and Accountability: Surround oneself with a supportive network of peers, mentors, or coaches who provide encouragement, feedback, and accountability. Sharing progress and challenges with others reinforces commitment and motivation.

Practice Self-Compassion: Be kind to oneself during setbacks or periods of low motivation. Acknowledge progress, celebrate achievements, and practice self-care to maintain overall well-being.

Stay Flexible and Adapt: Remain open to adjusting strategies, timelines, and goals based on evolving circumstances or feedback. Flexibility enables resilience and adaptability in the face of unforeseen challenges.

Consistency and motivation are integral components of the preparation journey, shaping the trajectory of success and fulfillment. By understanding the dynamics of consistency and motivation and implementing strategic approaches to sustain them, individuals can navigate challenges, overcome obstacles, and progress towards their goals with resilience and determination. Remember, the journey may be arduous at times, but each step forward brings one closer to realizing their aspirations and aspirations.

The Dream Deferred: *A Tale of Procrastination's Grip on a Young Entrepreneur*

Once upon a time, in a bustling city filled with dreams and opportunities, there lived a young entrepreneur named Alex. With a heart full of ambition and a mind brimming with ideas, Alex embarked on a journey to turn their passion into a thriving business.

As the sun rose on another promising day, Alex sat at their desk, surrounded by sketches, blueprints, and plans for their latest venture—an innovative startup that promised to revolutionize the tech industry. With boundless enthusiasm,

Alex dove into the project, fueled by visions of success and the promise of a brighter future.

However, as days turned into weeks and weeks into months, Alex found themselves falling prey to a familiar foe: procrastination. Despite their best intentions, tasks were pushed aside, deadlines were missed, and progress stagnated as procrastination tightened its suffocating grip.

At first, it was subtle—a fleeting distraction here, a minor delay there. But soon, procrastination morphed from a minor inconvenience into a formidable adversary, threatening to derail Alex's dreams before they could take flight.

Caught in the throes of procrastination, Alex struggled to regain control. Each day brought new excuses, new distractions, and new reasons to postpone progress. The once-clear path to success now seemed obscured by a dense fog of indecision and inertia.

As deadlines loomed and opportunities slipped through their fingers, Alex's confidence waned, replaced by a sense of frustration and self-doubt. The dream that once burned brightly in their heart now flickered weakly, threatened by the icy fingers of procrastination.

Despite their best efforts to break free, Alex found themselves trapped in a vicious cycle of procrastination and despair. The vision that once inspired them now seemed like a distant memory, overshadowed by the harsh reality of missed opportunities and unfulfilled potential.

In the end, it wasn't a lack of talent or ambition that thwarted Alex's dreams—it was the insidious grip of procrastination. As they watched their once-promising venture crumble before their eyes, Alex vowed to break free from procrastination's hold and reclaim their destiny.

And so, with renewed determination and a newfound resilience, Alex set out to conquer procrastination once and for all. Armed with perseverance, discipline, and a burning desire to succeed, they embarked on a journey to reignite the flame of their dreams and build a future filled with promise and possibility.

Though the road ahead was fraught with challenges, Alex refused to be deterred. For they knew that with unwavering commitment and a steadfast resolve, anything was possible. And so, with each step forward, Alex moved closer to realizing their dreams, leaving procrastination in the dust and embracing a future filled with boundless potential.

The Perilous Grip of Procrastination: *Overcoming the Deadly Disease of Delay*

Procrastination, the silent killer of dreams and productivity, affects millions worldwide. Despite its seemingly innocuous nature, procrastination exacts a heavy toll on mental health, productivity, and overall well-being. In this discourse, we'll delve into the roots of procrastination, its insidious effects, and actionable strategies to overcome its grip.

Understanding Procrastination:

At its core, procrastination is the act of delaying or postponing tasks, often in favor of more pleasurable or less demanding activities. While everyone procrastinates occasionally, chronic procrastination becomes a debilitating habit that impedes progress and stifles potential.

Root Causes of Procrastination:

Procrastination stems from various sources, including fear of failure, perfectionism, lack of motivation, poor time management skills, and even psychological factors such as anxiety or depression. Understanding the underlying causes is crucial in addressing and overcoming procrastination effectively.

The Toll of Procrastination:

Procrastination exacts a multifaceted toll on individuals and society at large. From missed deadlines and diminished productivity to increased stress and anxiety, the consequences of procrastination are far-reaching. Moreover, procrastination can erode self-esteem and hinder personal and professional growth, perpetuating a cycle of inertia and dissatisfaction.

Overcoming Procrastination:

While overcoming procrastination may seem daunting, it is entirely achievable with commitment and the right strategies.

 Follow these steps to combat procrastination:

Set Clear Goals: Establishing clear, achievable goals provides direction and motivation, making it easier to prioritize tasks and overcome procrastination.

Break Tasks into Manageable Steps: Breaking tasks into smaller, manageable steps makes them less daunting and more approachable, reducing the tendency to procrastinate.

Utilize Time Management Techniques: Techniques such as the Pomodoro Technique, time blocking, and prioritization can help improve focus and productivity, reducing the likelihood of procrastination.

Challenge Negative Thoughts: Addressing negative thought patterns, such as self-doubt or fear of failure, can mitigate the psychological barriers that contribute to procrastination.

Practice Self-Compassion: Cultivating self-compassion and acceptance fosters resilience and reduces the fear of making mistakes, making it easier to tackle tasks without succumbing to procrastination.

Create Accountability: Sharing goals with others or enlisting the support of a mentor or coach can provide accountability and encouragement, helping to overcome procrastination.

Celebrate Progress: Acknowledging and celebrating small victories along the way reinforces positive behavior and motivation, making it easier to stay on track and avoid procrastination.

Procrastination may be pervasive, but it is not insurmountable. By understanding its root causes, acknowledging its consequences, and implementing effective strategies, individuals can break free from the grip of procrastination and unlock their full potential. Remember, the journey to overcoming procrastination begins with a single step—take it today, and reclaim control over your time and destiny.

Chapter 5: Embracing Adaptability

The Art of Adaptability

In an ever-changing world, the ability to adapt is not just a valuable skill; it's a necessity for survival. From personal growth to professional success, adaptability plays a crucial role in how we navigate through life's myriad challenges and opportunities. In this exploration, we'll delve into the significance of adaptability, understanding its essence, and cultivating it in ourselves and others.

Adaptability is the capacity to adjust to new conditions and environments. It's the ability to remain flexible, open-minded, and resilient in the face of change. Whether it's a sudden shift in circumstances, a new challenge at work, or a major life transition, adaptable individuals possess the agility to respond effectively and thrive amidst uncertainty.

In today's fast-paced world, change is inevitable. Technological advancements, economic fluctuations, global crises, and personal developments constantly reshape our reality. Those who resist change risk being left behind, while those who embrace it find opportunities for growth and innovation. Adaptability is not just about survival; it's about seizing the moment and turning challenges into triumphs.

On a personal level, adaptability enables us to navigate life's ups and downs with resilience and grace. It empowers us to learn from setbacks, embrace new experiences, and evolve into the best versions of ourselves. By cultivating a growth mindset and embracing change as a catalyst for self-improvement, we can transform adversity into opportunity and chart a course toward personal fulfillment.

In the workplace, adaptability is a prized trait that sets high achievers apart. As industries evolve and job roles undergo transformation, those who can adapt quickly to new technologies, methodologies, and market dynamics are in high demand. Moreover, adaptable individuals are natural leaders who inspire confidence, drive innovation, and steer organizations toward success in turbulent times.

While some people seem naturally adaptable, adaptability is a skill that can be cultivated and honed over time.

Instead of resisting change, adopt a mindset of curiosity and openness. View change as an opportunity for growth and learning rather than a threat to your comfort zone.

Cultivate a flexible attitude and approach to life. Be willing to adjust your plans, priorities, and perspectives as circumstances evolve.

Strengthen your resilience by developing coping mechanisms, practicing self-care, and seeking support from others during challenging times.

Stay curious and committed to lifelong learning. Acquire new skills, knowledge, and experiences that enhance your adaptability and broaden your horizons.

Nurture your creative thinking skills to generate innovative solutions and approaches to problems. Embrace experimentation and embrace failure as a stepping stone to success.

Develop self-awareness, empathy, and interpersonal skills to navigate interpersonal dynamics and effectively collaborate with others in diverse environments.

Cultivate mindfulness practices such as meditation, yoga, or deep breathing exercises to stay grounded, present, and centered amidst chaos and uncertainty.

Solicit feedback from others to gain insights into your strengths, weaknesses, and blind spots. Use constructive feedback as a tool for self-improvement and growth.

Embrace change as a natural part of life and approach it with a positive attitude. Focus on what you can control, adapt to what you can't, and maintain a sense of optimism and resilience throughout the process.

Be a role model for adaptability by demonstrating flexibility, resilience, and openness to change in your words and actions. Inspire others to embrace change as an opportunity for growth and transformation.

In a world characterized by uncertainty and volatility, adaptability is the key to thriving amidst change. By cultivating the mindset, skills, and practices of adaptability, we can navigate life's twists and turns with resilience, grace, and confidence. Embrace change as a catalyst for growth, learn from every experience, and harness the power of adaptability to create a brighter, more resilient future for yourself and others.

Embracing Failure: The Crucial Path to Adaptability

In the pursuit of success, society often emphasizes the importance of winning, achieving, and excelling. However, amidst this celebration of success, the value of failure is frequently overlooked. Yet, it is through failure that some of life's most profound lessons are learned, and adaptability is honed. Learning from failures as the cornerstone of adaptability, exploring its psychological, emotional, and practical dimensions.

Failure, in its essence, is the outcome of falling short of expectations, goals, or desired outcomes. Whether in personal endeavors, professional pursuits, or academic aspirations, failure is an inevitable part of the human experience. Despite its negative connotations, failure presents an opportunity for growth, resilience, and transformation.

The psychological impact of failure can be profound, often triggering feelings of disappointment, frustration, and even shame. However, individuals who possess resilience view failure as a stepping stone rather than a stumbling block. By reframing failure as a learning opportunity, individuals can cultivate psychological resilience, enabling them to bounce back stronger and more determined than before.

One of the greatest barriers to learning from failure is the fear of vulnerability. Many individuals perceive failure as a reflection of their inadequacies or shortcomings, leading to avoidance or denial. However, embracing vulnerability is essential in the process of self-discovery and growth. By acknowledging their failures and vulnerabilities, individuals can confront them head-on, leading to greater self-awareness and personal development.

Central to the process of learning from failure is reflection. Instead of dismissing failures as mere setbacks, individuals are encouraged to engage in introspection, analyzing the root causes, underlying factors, and potential areas for improvement. Through reflective practices such as journaling, feedback seeking, and mentorship, individuals can extract valuable insights from their failures, paving the way for future success.

Adaptability in Action:

Adaptability, often defined as the ability to adjust to new conditions or circumstances, is intrinsically linked to the capacity to learn from failure. In a rapidly changing world, where uncertainty and unpredictability abound, adaptability is a critical skill for navigating challenges and seizing opportunities. By embracing failure as a natural part of the learning process, individuals can enhance their adaptability quotient, enabling them to thrive in dynamic environments.

Numerous examples from various domains illustrate the transformative power of learning from failure. From the innovative experiments of Thomas Edison, whose numerous attempts led to the invention of the light bulb, to the resilience of J.K. Rowling, who faced rejection before achieving literary success with Harry Potter, these stories exemplify the triumph of perseverance, resilience, and adaptability in the face of adversity.

Educational Implications:

In the realm of education, fostering a culture that values and embraces failure is paramount. By shifting the focus from grades and standardized testing to the process of learning and growth, educators can empower students to take risks, experiment, and learn from their mistakes. Encouraging a growth mindset, wherein failure is viewed as an opportunity for improvement rather than a mark of incompetence, can cultivate resilience, creativity, and adaptability in students.

 Learning from failure is not merely a desirable trait but a vital necessity in today's ever-changing world. By reframing failure as a catalyst for growth, individuals can cultivate psychological resilience, embrace vulnerability, and enhance their adaptability quotient. Through reflective practices, adaptive learning, and a willingness to embrace vulnerability, individuals can transform setbacks into stepping stones, ultimately achieving greater success and fulfillment in life.

Flexibility

Flexibility is indeed a crucial component of effective preparation, whether it pertains to personal goals, professional endeavors, or even unexpected life events. In today's rapidly changing world, the ability to adapt and adjust one's plans in response to new information or circumstances is often the difference between success and failure.

One area where flexibility plays a significant role is in career planning. Gone are the days of pursuing a single career path for an entire lifetime. With technological advancements, globalization, and shifting market demands, the job landscape is in a constant state of flux. Therefore, individuals must be prepared to pivot and explore alternative avenues when necessary. This might involve acquiring new skills, seeking out different opportunities, or even changing industries altogether. By embracing flexibility, individuals can navigate the uncertainties of the job market with greater ease and resilience.

Moreover, flexibility is essential in educational pursuits. While having a clear plan and set goals is important, it is equally important to remain open to new learning experiences and opportunities for growth. For instance, a student may enter college with a specific major in mind, only to discover a passion for a completely different field of study. By remaining flexible and open-minded, they can adjust their academic trajectory accordingly, ultimately finding fulfillment and success in their chosen path.

In the realm of entrepreneurship and business, flexibility is paramount. Startups, in particular, often face numerous challenges and obstacles along the path to success. Entrepreneurs must be willing to iterate on their ideas, pivot their business models, and adapt to changing market conditions. Those who are rigid and unwilling to deviate from their original plan are at a distinct disadvantage. By contrast, entrepreneurs who embrace flexibility can more effectively respond to feedback, seize new opportunities, and ultimately increase their chances of success.

Furthermore, flexibility is essential in personal relationships. Whether it's with friends, family, or romantic partners, being adaptable and willing to compromise is key to fostering healthy and harmonious connections. Life is unpredictable, and unforeseen circumstances can put strain on even the strongest of relationships. By practicing flexibility and empathy, individuals can navigate conflicts more effectively, strengthen their bonds with others, and cultivate deeper, more meaningful connections.

In addition to its practical benefits, flexibility also contributes to overall well-being and resilience. Research has shown that individuals who possess greater psychological flexibility— defined as the ability to adapt to changing situational demands and to shift one's mindset when necessary—are better equipped to cope with stress, navigate life transitions, and maintain emotional balance. By cultivating this trait, individuals can not only weather life's ups and downs more effectively but also experience greater satisfaction and fulfillment in their daily lives.

Flexibility is a key component of effective preparation in all areas of life. Whether it's in career planning, educational pursuits, entrepreneurship, personal relationships, or overall well-being, the ability to adapt and adjust to changing circumstances is essential for success and fulfillment. By embracing flexibility, individuals can navigate the uncertainties of life with greater ease, resilience, and optimism, ultimately achieving their goals and realizing their full potential.

Flexibility helps in the preparation stage

Flexibility is a crucial attribute in the preparation stage across various domains, including business, education, sports, and personal development.

Flexibility in preparation is akin to a safety net, providing the ability to adapt to changing circumstances, unexpected challenges, or new opportunities. In the context of business, a flexible approach to preparation enables companies to pivot their strategies in response to market fluctuations, technological advancements, or shifts in consumer preferences. For example, during the COVID-19 pandemic, businesses that were able to quickly adapt their operations, supply chains, and marketing strategies to accommodate remote work and changing consumer behaviors were better positioned to survive and thrive.

In education, flexibility in preparation allows educators to tailor their teaching methods to suit the diverse learning styles and needs of students. It involves being open to incorporating new teaching techniques, technologies, or resources to enhance student engagement and learning outcomes. Additionally, flexible preparation enables educators to adjust their lesson plans based on student feedback, assessment results, or emerging trends in education.

In sports, preparation is key to achieving peak performance, and flexibility plays a vital role in optimizing training regimens, tactics, and mindset. Athletes and coaches must be willing to adapt their training plans based on factors such as injuries, weather conditions, or changes in competition schedules. Flexibility also extends to mental preparation, where athletes learn to manage stress, overcome setbacks, and stay focused amidst distractions.

On a personal level, flexibility in preparation involves being open-minded, adaptable, and resilient in pursuing goals and navigating life's challenges. It means having the ability to adjust plans, priorities, and timelines in response to changing circumstances or unforeseen obstacles. This might involve reevaluating career goals, making lifestyle changes, or embracing new opportunities that arise unexpectedly.

One of the primary benefits of flexibility in the preparation stage is its ability to foster innovation and creativity. When individuals or organizations are open to exploring different approaches, experimenting with new ideas, and taking calculated risks, they are more likely to discover novel solutions and achieve breakthroughs. This can lead to competitive advantages, improved performance, and long-term success.

Flexibility also promotes agility, which is essential in today's fast-paced and ever-changing world. By being adaptable and responsive, individuals and organizations can quickly seize opportunities, overcome challenges, and stay ahead of the curve. This agility enables them to thrive in dynamic environments where uncertainty and volatility are the norm.

Moreover, flexibility in preparation enhances resilience, enabling individuals and organizations to bounce back from setbacks and adversity. Instead of being rigidly attached to a specific plan or outcome, they are able to pivot, regroup, and persevere in the face of obstacles. This resilience is a key factor in long-term success and sustainability.

However, while flexibility is valuable, it is essential to strike a balance between adaptability and consistency. While it's important to be open to change and innovation, it's also crucial to maintain a sense of stability and focus. Too much flexibility can lead to indecision, inconsistency, or a lack of direction, undermining progress and effectiveness.

 Flexibility in the preparation stage is a critical attribute that enables individuals and organizations to adapt, innovate, and thrive in today's dynamic world. By being open-minded, adaptable, and resilient, they can overcome challenges, seize opportunities, and achieve success. Whether in business, education, sports, or personal development, flexibility is a key factor in achieving peak performance and long-term sustainability.

Chapter 6: Building a Support System

Creating a supportive network of friends, family, and mentors is crucial in the preparation period for any endeavor, whether it's pursuing a career, starting a business, or achieving personal goals. This network acts as a safety net, providing emotional support, guidance, and encouragement during times of uncertainty and challenges.

Let's delve into why this support system is so important and how it can impact an individual's success.

The Power of Emotional Support

During the preparation phase, individuals often face moments of self-doubt, anxiety, and stress. Having a supportive network can alleviate these feelings by providing emotional reassurance and understanding. Friends and family members who genuinely care about one's well-being can offer a listening ear, offer perspective, and remind the individual of their strengths and capabilities. This emotional support can boost confidence and motivation, enabling the individual to stay focused and committed to their goals.

Guidance and Advice

Mentors play a crucial role in providing guidance and advice during the preparation period. These are individuals who have experience and expertise in the field the individual is entering. They can offer valuable insights, share their own experiences, and provide practical tips on how to navigate challenges and obstacles. Mentors can also help individuals set realistic goals, develop action plans, and stay accountable for their progress. Their wisdom and guidance can significantly accelerate the learning curve and increase the likelihood of success.

Networking Opportunities

A supportive network also opens doors to valuable networking opportunities. Friends, family members, and mentors may have connections in the industry or know someone who can provide additional support or resources. Networking allows individuals to expand their circle of influence, gain access to new opportunities, and learn from others who have achieved success in similar endeavors. By leveraging the connections within their network, individuals can tap into a wealth of knowledge and support that can help propel them forward in their journey.

Motivation and Accountability

In moments of doubt or procrastination, having a supportive network can serve as a source of motivation and accountability. Friends and family members who believe in the individual's potential can offer words of encouragement and remind them of their goals and aspirations. Likewise, mentors can hold individuals accountable for their actions, providing gentle nudges or constructive criticism when needed. This external motivation can help individuals stay on track and overcome challenges with renewed determination.

Celebrating Successes

Finally, a supportive network celebrates the successes and milestones achieved during the preparation period. Whether it's landing a job interview, completing a challenging project, or reaching a personal milestone, friends, family members, and mentors are there to cheer on the individual's accomplishments. This recognition not only boosts morale but also reinforces the individual's belief in their abilities and the value of their hard work and dedication.

Surrounding oneself with a supportive network of friends, family, and mentors is essential during the preparation period for any endeavor. This network provides emotional support, guidance, networking opportunities, motivation, and accountability, all of which are crucial for success. By cultivating strong relationships and leveraging the expertise and connections within their network, individuals can navigate challenges, accelerate their progress, and ultimately achieve their goals.

Seeking guidance and advice

Seeking guidance and advice from experienced individuals is crucial, especially in the preparation stage of any endeavor.

In any field or endeavor, whether it's starting a business, pursuing a career, or mastering a skill, preparation is key to success. However, navigating the complexities of preparation can be daunting, especially for those who are new to the endeavor. This is where the wisdom and guidance of experienced individuals become invaluable. Drawing from their wealth of experiences, they can provide insights, advice, and mentorship that can greatly enhance your preparation process and increase your chances of success.

Why Seeking Guidance and Advice is Important:

Avoiding Common Pitfalls:

One of the primary benefits of seeking guidance from experienced individuals is the ability to avoid common pitfalls and mistakes. In any field, there are certain challenges and obstacles that are likely to arise during the preparation stage. By learning from the experiences of others, you can identify these potential pitfalls early on and take proactive measures to mitigate them.

For example, imagine you are preparing to launch a new product in the market. An experienced entrepreneur who has previously launched similar products can provide valuable insights into the challenges they faced, such as pricing strategies, distribution channels, and customer feedback. By heeding their advice, you can avoid making the same mistakes and increase the likelihood of a successful product launch.

Gaining Practical Insights:

Experienced individuals possess practical insights and knowledge that cannot be gained from textbooks or theoretical learning alone. They have firsthand experience dealing with real-world scenarios, navigating challenges, and finding solutions.

For instance, if you are preparing to enter the field of finance, seeking guidance from a seasoned financial analyst can provide you with practical insights into market trends, investment strategies, and risk management techniques. Their experiences can help you develop a deeper understanding of the industry and equip you with the skills necessary to excel in your career.

Mentoring and Support:

Mentoring plays a crucial role in the preparation stage, as it provides individuals with personalized guidance, support, and encouragement. Experienced mentors can offer valuable advice, share their own experiences, and provide constructive feedback to help you navigate the complexities of preparation.

Consider the example of a budding entrepreneur who is preparing to launch a tech startup. By seeking mentorship from an experienced business leader in the tech industry, they can receive personalized guidance on various aspects of preparation, such as product development, marketing strategies, and fundraising techniques. The mentor can also offer emotional support during challenging times and help the individual stay focused on their goals.

Expanding Your Network:

Another benefit of seeking guidance from experienced individuals is the opportunity to expand your network and connect with industry professionals. Networking plays a crucial role in the preparation stage, as it allows you to learn from others, exchange ideas, and explore potential opportunities.

For example, if you are preparing to transition into a new career field, connecting with experienced professionals through networking events, industry conferences, or online forums can provide you with valuable insights and resources. These connections can also open doors to new opportunities, such as job offers, internships, or mentorship opportunities.

Building Confidence and Resilience:

Lastly, seeking guidance from experienced individuals can help build your confidence and resilience during the preparation stage. Knowing that you have the support and guidance of someone who has successfully navigated similar challenges can boost your confidence and give you the courage to overcome obstacles.

Imagine you are preparing to pursue a challenging academic program. By seeking guidance from former students who have successfully completed the program, you can gain valuable advice on study techniques, time management strategies, and exam preparation tips. Their encouragement and support can help you stay motivated and resilient, even in the face of adversity.

Seeking guidance and advice from experienced individuals is paramount in the preparation stage of any endeavor. Whether you are starting a business, pursuing a career, or mastering a skill, the wisdom and insights of those who have gone before you can greatly enhance your preparation process and increase your chances of success. By learning from their experiences, avoiding common pitfalls, gaining practical insights, receiving mentoring and support, expanding your network, and building confidence and resilience, you can navigate the complexities of preparation more effectively and achieve your goals with greater confidence and success.

Preparation with Collaboration

Collaboration in the preparation stage is fundamental for enhancing knowledge, experience, and performance. Whether in academic endeavors, professional projects, or personal development, working with others can significantly enrich the process and outcomes.

Collaboration is more than just working together; it's about leveraging diverse perspectives, pooling resources, and achieving collective goals. In the preparation stage, collaboration lays the foundation for success by fostering creativity, sharing expertise, and building supportive networks.

Education

In academic settings, collaboration is a cornerstone of learning. Group projects, discussions, and peer review processes encourage students to engage with different ideas, challenge their assumptions, and develop critical thinking skills. Collaborating with classmates also enables students to tap into each other's strengths, whether it's research skills, presentation abilities, or subject matter expertise. Through collaboration, students not only deepen their understanding of the material but also learn valuable interpersonal skills such as communication, negotiation, and teamwork.

Business

In the business world, collaboration is essential for driving innovation and achieving strategic objectives. Cross-functional teams bring together individuals with diverse backgrounds and expertise to tackle complex challenges. By sharing knowledge and resources, team members can generate new ideas, identify opportunities, and develop creative solutions. Collaboration also fosters a culture of trust and accountability, where team members feel empowered to take risks and experiment with new approaches. In today's rapidly changing business environment, collaboration enables organizations to adapt quickly to market dynamics and stay ahead of the competition.

Personal Growth

Collaboration is not limited to formal settings; it also plays a crucial role in personal growth and development. Whether pursuing a hobby, learning a new skill, or tackling a passion project, collaborating with others can accelerate progress and enrich the experience. Joining communities, attending workshops, and seeking mentorship provide opportunities to learn from others, receive feedback, and expand one's horizons. Collaboration also fosters a sense of belonging and connection, as individuals come together around shared interests and goals. By collaborating with others, individuals can achieve more than they could on their own and experience personal growth in the process.

Challenges and Solutions

While collaboration offers numerous benefits, it also presents challenges that must be navigated effectively. Communication breakdowns, conflicting priorities, and personality clashes can impede progress and undermine team cohesion. To address these challenges, it's essential to establish clear goals, roles, and expectations from the outset. Regular check-ins, feedback sessions, and conflict resolution mechanisms can also help keep collaboration on track and foster a positive working environment. Additionally, leveraging technology tools such as project management software, video conferencing platforms, and collaborative documents can facilitate communication and coordination among team members, regardless of location or time zone.

Collaboration is indispensable in the preparation stage for enhancing knowledge, experience, and performance. Whether in education, business, or personal growth, working with others enables individuals to tap into diverse perspectives, share expertise, and achieve collective goals. By fostering collaboration, we can unlock creativity, drive innovation, and build stronger, more resilient communities. As we navigate an increasingly interconnected and complex world, collaboration will continue to be a cornerstone of success in the preparation stage and beyond.

Chapter 7: Mental and Emotional Preparation

Mental and Emotional Preparation: The Cornerstone of Success

The process of preparing for any significant endeavor—whether it be a competitive exam, a major project at work, or an athletic competition—requires not only physical and intellectual readiness but also mental and emotional preparation. The latter is often overlooked, yet it forms the foundation upon which all other forms of preparation rest. Without mental and emotional stability, even the most well-prepared individuals can falter.

The Importance of Mental and Emotional Preparation

Mental and emotional preparation involves conditioning the mind and emotions to handle the stresses, pressures, and challenges that accompany any major task. This preparation can include developing resilience, cultivating a positive mindset, and employing strategies to manage anxiety and stress.

Resilience and Coping Strategies

Resilience is the ability to recover quickly from difficulties. It is a crucial component of mental preparation because setbacks and failures are inevitable in any significant endeavor. For example, consider an athlete training for the Olympics. Despite rigorous physical training, injuries or poor performances in preliminary competitions can be demoralizing. However, an athlete with strong mental resilience can bounce back from these setbacks, using them as learning experiences rather than letting them derail their overall objective. They might employ coping strategies such as visualization, where they imagine themselves overcoming obstacles and achieving their goals, thereby maintaining motivation and focus.

Positive Mindset and Self-belief

A positive mindset and self-belief are fundamental to mental preparation. These attributes help individuals to remain optimistic and confident in their abilities, even when faced with challenges. For instance, a student preparing for a highly competitive entrance exam may face immense pressure and doubt. By fostering a positive mindset and believing in their capabilities, the student can approach their studies with enthusiasm and persistence. Techniques such as affirmations—repeatedly telling oneself that they are capable and prepared—can reinforce this positive mindset.

Stress and Anxiety Management

Managing stress and anxiety is another critical aspect of mental and emotional preparation. High levels of stress can impair cognitive functions and performance. For example, in high-stakes professions like surgery, the ability to remain calm and composed under pressure is essential. Surgeons often undergo rigorous training not just in technical skills but also in stress management techniques, such as deep breathing exercises and mindfulness meditation, to ensure they can perform optimally even in high-pressure situations.

Examples Illustrating Mental and Emotional Preparation

To illustrate the significance of mental and emotional preparation, let's delve into specific examples across different fields: academics, sports, and professional careers.

Academic Excellence: The Story of Malala Yousafzai

Malala Yousafzai, the youngest-ever Nobel Prize laureate, is an exemplary figure in demonstrating the power of mental and emotional preparation. Growing up in Pakistan, Malala faced severe threats and violence from the Taliban for advocating girls' education. Despite these challenges, she remained mentally strong and emotionally resilient. Her ability to maintain a positive outlook and unwavering belief in her cause, even after surviving an assassination attempt, allowed her to continue her advocacy on a global scale. Malala's story underscores how mental and emotional fortitude can empower individuals to overcome extreme adversities and achieve extraordinary goals.

Athletic Achievement: Michael Phelps' Olympic Journey

Michael Phelps, the most decorated Olympian of all time, credits much of his success to mental preparation. Phelps worked with a sports psychologist to develop mental strategies that enhanced his performance. Visualization was a key component of his preparation; he would mentally rehearse his races in vivid detail, imagining every stroke and turn. This mental rehearsal helped him to remain calm and focused during actual competitions, effectively reducing performance anxiety. Phelps' meticulous mental preparation was instrumental in his ability to consistently perform at the highest level and achieve his record-breaking successes.

Professional Success: The Leadership of Angela Merkel

Angela Merkel, the former Chancellor of Germany, exemplifies the role of mental and emotional preparation in leadership. Leading a country through multiple crises, including the 2008 financial crisis and the European migrant crisis, required not only strategic acumen but also immense emotional resilience. Merkel's ability to remain composed, make informed decisions under pressure, and communicate effectively with both her government and the public was crucial. Her emotional intelligence—understanding and managing her own emotions, as well as empathizing with others—played a significant role in her leadership success.

Strategies for Mental and Emotional Preparation

Given the importance of mental and emotional preparation, what strategies can individuals adopt to cultivate these attributes? Here are some effective methods:

Mindfulness and Meditation

Mindfulness practices, including meditation, help individuals to stay present and reduce stress. Regular mindfulness practice can enhance emotional regulation, improve focus, and increase resilience. For example, incorporating a daily meditation routine can help students manage exam-related stress and improve their concentration.

Visualization and Mental Rehearsal

Visualization involves creating a mental image of success. Athletes, performers, and professionals can use visualization to mentally rehearse their tasks, which can boost confidence and reduce anxiety. This technique prepares the mind to handle real-life situations more effectively.

Cognitive Behavioral Techniques

Cognitive Behavioral Therapy (CBT) techniques can help individuals to reframe negative thoughts and develop a more positive mindset. By identifying and challenging unhelpful thought patterns, individuals can reduce anxiety and build self-belief. For example, a professional facing a daunting project can use CBT techniques to transform thoughts of doubt into affirmations of capability and preparedness.

Support Systems

Building a robust support system is essential for emotional preparation. Friends, family, mentors, and coaches can provide encouragement, advice, and perspective. Engaging with a supportive community can help individuals to manage stress and maintain motivation.

Goal Setting and Planning

Setting clear, achievable goals and creating a structured plan to achieve them can enhance mental preparedness. Breaking down larger tasks into smaller, manageable steps can make the overall goal seem less overwhelming and more attainable. This approach also provides a sense of progress and accomplishment, which can boost motivation.

Self-care and Physical Health

Mental and emotional well-being are closely linked to physical health. Regular exercise, a balanced diet, and adequate sleep are fundamental to maintaining mental clarity and emotional stability. regular physical activity has been shown to reduce symptoms of depression and anxiety, enhancing overall well-being.

Mental and emotional preparation is the cornerstone of success across various fields. Whether in academics, sports, or professional careers, the ability to manage stress, maintain a positive mindset, and exhibit resilience is crucial. By employing strategies such as mindfulness, visualization, cognitive behavioral techniques, building support systems, goal setting, and self-care, individuals can enhance their mental and emotional readiness. As illustrated by the examples of Malala Yousafzai, Michael Phelps, and Angela Merkel, those who invest in their mental and emotional preparation are better equipped to overcome challenges and achieve their goals. Thus, mental and emotional preparation is not just beneficial but essential for success in any significant endeavor.

The common symptom in preparation stage

Stress and anxiety are common experiences during the preparation process for various endeavors, whether academic exams, professional certifications, or significant life events. This comprehensive exploration of the topic aims to illustrate these experiences and provide strategies for managing them, ultimately fostering motivation and resilience.

Understanding Stress and Anxiety

1. *Definition and Symptoms*

Stress is a response to a perceived threat or challenge, resulting in physiological changes such as increased heart rate and muscle tension. Anxiety, while often used interchangeably with stress, is a more persistent condition characterized by excessive worry, nervousness, and fear. Symptoms of both can include:

Physical: Headaches, fatigue, insomnia, digestive issues.

Emotional: Irritability, mood swings, feelings of overwhelm.

Cognitive: Difficulty concentrating, forgetfulness, negative thinking.

Behavioral: Procrastination, avoidance, changes in eating or sleeping patterns.

2. *Causes of Stress and Anxiety in Preparation*

Common triggers during the preparation process include:

High Expectations: Setting unrealistic goals can lead to feelings of inadequacy.

Fear of Failure: The pressure to succeed can create a fear of disappointing oneself or others.

Time Constraints: Balancing preparation with other responsibilities can be overwhelming.

Lack of Control: Uncertainty about the outcome can exacerbate anxiety.

Social Comparison: Comparing oneself to peers can lead to self-doubt and competitive stress.

Impact of Stress and Anxiety on Performance

While a moderate amount of stress can be motivating and improve focus, excessive stress and anxiety can hinder performance. Chronic stress impairs cognitive functions, reducing the ability to concentrate, process information, and make decisions. Anxiety can lead to avoidance behaviors, further delaying progress and reinforcing negative self-perceptions.

Strategies to Manage Stress and Anxiety

1. Practical Techniques

Time Management: Create a realistic study or preparation schedule. Break tasks into manageable chunks and prioritize them. Use tools like calendars, planners, or apps to stay organized.

Healthy Lifestyle: Maintain a balanced diet, regular exercise, and adequate sleep. Physical health directly impacts mental well-being.

Relaxation Techniques: Practice mindfulness, meditation, or deep breathing exercises to calm the mind and reduce physiological symptoms of stress.

Positive Environment: Create a conducive study environment free from distractions. Surround yourself with supportive and positive influences.

2. Cognitive Strategies

Positive Affirmations: Replace negative thoughts with positive affirmations. Remind yourself of past successes and your capabilities.

Reframing: Shift your perspective on stress by viewing challenges as opportunities for growth rather than threats.

Goal Setting: Set SMART (Specific, Measurable, Achievable, Relevant, Time-bound) goals. This provides clear direction and a sense of achievement as you progress.

Self-Compassion: Practice self-compassion by being kind to yourself during setbacks. Recognize that everyone experiences difficulties and that it's a normal part of the process.

3. *Social Support*

Peer Support: Engage with peers who are also preparing. Sharing experiences and strategies can be reassuring and motivating.

Professional Help: If anxiety becomes overwhelming, consider seeking help from a counselor or therapist. Professional guidance can provide coping mechanisms and emotional support.

Communication: Keep open lines of communication with family and friends. Expressing your feelings can alleviate some of the burden.

Inspirational Stories

1. *Academic Success*

Consider the story of Malala Yousafzai, who faced immense challenges, including life-threatening dangers, in her pursuit of education. Despite these obstacles, she remained steadfast in her goals, eventually becoming the youngest Nobel Prize laureate. Her resilience and determination serve as a powerful reminder that persistence in the face of stress and anxiety can lead to remarkable achievements.

2. Professional Achievements

Steve Jobs, co-founder of Apple Inc., faced numerous setbacks, including being ousted from the very company he helped build. Instead of succumbing to stress and anxiety, he used the experience to fuel his creativity, founding NeXT and acquiring Pixar, before returning to Apple and leading it to unprecedented success. His journey underscores the importance of resilience and viewing setbacks as opportunities for growth.

3. Personal Triumphs

J.K. Rowling, the author of the Harry Potter series, experienced significant personal and financial struggles before her success. Despite these challenges, she continued writing and persevered through numerous rejections from publishers. Her story illustrates that perseverance and belief in oneself, even when faced with considerable adversity, can lead to extraordinary outcomes.

Motivational Techniques

1. Visualization

Visualization is a powerful tool to enhance motivation and reduce anxiety. By imagining yourself successfully completing your tasks or achieving your goals, you create a mental roadmap that can increase confidence and focus.

2. Incremental Progress

Recognize and celebrate small victories along the way. Each completed task brings you closer to your goal and provides a sense of accomplishment that can motivate you to keep going.

3. Intrinsic Motivation

Find personal meaning and intrinsic motivation in your preparation. Whether it's a passion for the subject, a desire to improve your skills, or a personal goal, connecting with your internal drive can sustain your motivation even during challenging times.

4. Accountability

Set up accountability mechanisms, such as study groups or regular check-ins with a mentor. Knowing that others are aware of your goals and progress can provide additional motivation to stay on track.

Stress and anxiety are common companions on the journey of preparation, but they do not have to be overwhelming obstacles. By understanding their causes and impacts, and by implementing effective strategies for management, individuals can transform these challenges into opportunities for growth and success. Through practical techniques, cognitive reframing, social support, and inspirational examples, it is possible to navigate the pressures of preparation with resilience and determination.

Embrace the process, trust in your abilities, and remember that every step taken, no matter how small, brings you closer to your goal. Stay motivated, stay focused, and most importantly, believe in yourself. The journey may be demanding, but the rewards of perseverance and dedication are well worth the effort.

Strategies for managing stress and anxiety .

Managing stress and anxiety effectively often involves a combination of lifestyle changes, mental health practices, and professional support.

Adopting few steps can reduce stress and anxiety.

Lifestyle Changes

Regular Exercise: Physical activity can boost your mood and reduce stress hormones.

Healthy Diet: Eating a balanced diet can improve your overall health and mood.

Adequate Sleep: Ensure you get 7-9 hours of quality sleep each night.

Limit Stimulants: Reduce caffeine and alcohol intake, as they can increase anxiety.

Mental Health Practices

Mindfulness and Meditation: Practices like mindfulness meditation can help calm the mind and reduce stress.

Breathing Exercises: Techniques such as deep breathing can help you relax.

Positive Thinking: Challenge negative thoughts and focus on positive aspects of your life.

Time Management: Prioritize tasks and break them into manageable steps to avoid feeling overwhelmed.

Professional Support

Therapy: Cognitive-behavioral therapy (CBT) and other forms of counseling can be very effective.

Medication: For some, medication prescribed by a healthcare provider can help manage anxiety.

Support Groups: Joining a support group can provide a sense of community and understanding.

Daily Practices

Stay Connected: Maintain social connections with friends and family.

Hobbies and Interests: Engage in activities you enjoy to take your mind off stress.

Limit News Consumption: Reduce exposure to distressing news, especially before bed.

Set Boundaries: Learn to say no to demands that cause excessive stress.

Relaxation Techniques

Progressive Muscle Relaxation: Tense and then slowly relax different muscle groups.

Yoga: Combines physical postures, breathing exercises, and meditation.

Nature Walks: Spending time in nature can be very soothing.

Implementing these strategies can help create a balanced approach to managing stress and anxiety. It's important to find what works best for you and to seek professional help if needed.

Cultivating a positive mindset

Cultivating a positive mindset during the preparation stage is crucial for success in any endeavor, whether it be academic, professional, or personal. Lets explore the importance of a positive mindset, providing detailed examples and strategies for developing and maintaining such an outlook. We'll examine the psychological underpinnings of positivity, the role of motivation and resilience, and practical techniques to foster a positive mindset.

The Importance of a Positive Mindset

A positive mindset, characterized by optimism, resilience, and a proactive approach to challenges, can significantly enhance performance and well-being. This outlook enables individuals to view obstacles as opportunities, maintain motivation, and persist through difficulties.

Psychological Underpinnings

Optimism and Success: Research has consistently shown that optimism is linked to better outcomes in various fields. Optimistic individuals are more likely to set and achieve goals because they believe in their ability to influence events in their lives.

Resilience and Stress Management: A positive mindset enhances resilience, allowing individuals to recover from setbacks more quickly. This is crucial during the preparation stage, where challenges and failures are inevitable.

Role of Motivation and Resilience

Motivation and resilience are critical components of a positive mindset. They enable individuals to sustain effort and bounce back from setbacks, respectively.

Intrinsic vs. Extrinsic Motivation

Intrinsic Motivation: This refers to engaging in an activity for its own sake, driven by interest and enjoyment. For example, a student who enjoys learning is more likely to persist in their studies despite difficulties.

Extrinsic Motivation: This involves external rewards or recognition. While effective in the short term, it is often less sustainable. A professional preparing for a certification may be motivated by the potential for career advancement and higher salary.

Building Resilience

Resilience can be built through various strategies:

Growth Mindset: Embracing a growth mindset, as proposed by Carol Dweck, involves believing that abilities can be developed through dedication and hard work. This contrasts with a fixed mindset, which views abilities as static.

Positive Self-Talk: Replacing negative thoughts with positive affirmations can build resilience. For instance, instead of thinking "I can't do this," one might say, "I can improve with practice."

Strategies for Cultivating a Positive Mindset

Cultivating a positive mindset involves intentional practices and habits.

Setting Realistic Goals

Setting achievable goals is crucial. Unrealistic goals can lead to frustration and a negative mindset. Breaking down larger goals into smaller, manageable tasks can make the preparation process less daunting and more rewarding.

Example: A student preparing for a major exam can break down their study schedule into daily or weekly goals, focusing on specific topics or chapters. This approach provides a sense of accomplishment and keeps motivation high.

Visualization and Affirmations

Visualization involves imagining oneself successfully completing a task, which can enhance motivation and performance. Affirmations are positive statements that reinforce a positive self-image and confidence.

Example: An athlete preparing for a competition might visualize themselves performing at their best, crossing the finish line, or winning the match. They might use affirmations like "I am strong and capable."

Mindfulness and Meditation

Mindfulness practices help in maintaining focus and reducing stress. Meditation can enhance awareness and control over one's thoughts, fostering a positive mindset.

Example: A professional preparing for a critical presentation might engage in daily mindfulness meditation to reduce anxiety and increase concentration.

Positive Social Support

Surrounding oneself with supportive and positive individuals can have a profound impact on mindset. Positive social interactions provide encouragement, constructive feedback, and a sense of belonging.

Example: An entrepreneur preparing to launch a new business might join a support group or network with other entrepreneurs to share experiences and gain encouragement.

Practical Techniques to Foster a Positive Mindset

Implementing practical techniques in daily routines can reinforce a positive mindset:

Gratitude Journaling

Maintaining a gratitude journal involves writing down things one is thankful for each day. This practice shifts focus from negative aspects to positive experiences.

Example: A student facing the pressures of academic life can benefit from jotting down daily successes and moments of gratitude, such as a productive study session or support from a friend.

Physical Activity

Regular exercise has been shown to improve mood and reduce anxiety. Physical activity releases endorphins, which are natural mood lifters.

Example: A professional preparing for an important project might incorporate a daily workout routine to stay physically and mentally fit.

Balanced Lifestyle

A balanced lifestyle that includes proper nutrition, adequate sleep, and leisure activities supports a positive mindset. Neglecting these areas can lead to burnout and negative thinking.

Example: An artist preparing for a gallery exhibition should ensure they are eating well, getting enough rest, and taking breaks to engage in enjoyable activities, preventing creative fatigue.

Case Studies and Real-Life Examples

To illustrate the impact of a positive mindset, we will explore several case studies:

Academic Success: The Story of Malala Yousafzai

Malala Yousafzai, the youngest Nobel Prize laureate, exemplifies the power of a positive mindset in the face of extreme adversity. Despite being shot by the Taliban for advocating girls' education, she remained resilient and optimistic. Her unwavering belief in the importance of education and her determination to overcome obstacles have inspired millions worldwide.

Professional Achievement: Oprah Winfrey

Oprah Winfrey's journey from a challenging childhood to becoming one of the most influential media moguls in the world demonstrates the importance of a positive mindset. Despite numerous setbacks, her perseverance, self-belief, and positive outlook enabled her to achieve extraordinary success.

Personal Development: J.K. Rowling

J.K. Rowling's story of going from living on welfare to becoming a best-selling author of the Harry Potter series is a testament to resilience and a positive mindset. She faced numerous rejections from publishers but continued to believe in her work and its potential impact.

Cultivating a positive mindset during the preparation stage is essential for achieving success and personal growth. It involves embracing optimism, building resilience, setting realistic goals, and engaging in practices such as visualization, mindfulness, and gratitude journaling. Through the examples of individuals like Malala Yousafzai, Oprah Winfrey, and J.K. Rowling, we see the transformative power of a positive outlook.

By incorporating these strategies and techniques, individuals can enhance their motivation, manage stress more effectively, and navigate the challenges of the preparation stage with greater confidence and success. A positive mindset not only improves performance but also contributes to overall well-being and life satisfaction.

The Deep Connection Between Mental Well-Being and Preparedness

Mental well-being and preparedness are intertwined in a relationship that significantly impacts an individual's ability to navigate life's challenges. Preparedness, in this context, refers to the state of being ready and able to respond effectively to various situations, whether they are daily tasks, unexpected crises, or long-term goals. This readiness can manifest in numerous forms, including emotional resilience, cognitive flexibility, practical planning, and physical health. Understanding the connection between mental well-being and preparedness is crucial for fostering a holistic approach to health that supports individuals in leading balanced, fulfilling lives.

The Concept of Mental Well-Being

Mental well-being is a multifaceted concept encompassing emotional, psychological, and social aspects. It includes how individuals think, feel, and act, and is influenced by a range of factors including biology, environment, and personal experiences. Key components of mental well-being include:

Emotional Health: The ability to manage and express emotions appropriately.

Psychological Resilience: The capacity to recover from setbacks and maintain a stable mental state.

Social Well-being: Healthy relationships and effective communication skills.

Cognitive Functioning: The ability to think clearly, make decisions, and solve problems.

Defining Preparedness

Preparedness involves being ready and able to handle various situations, both expected and unexpected. It can be broken down into several domains:

Practical Preparedness: Having plans and resources in place for potential emergencies.

Emotional Preparedness: Developing resilience and coping mechanisms to manage stress and emotional upheavals.

Cognitive Preparedness: Cultivating a mindset that is flexible, adaptable, and solution-oriented.

Physical Preparedness: Maintaining physical health and fitness to support overall well-being.

The Link Between Mental Well-Being and Preparedness

The relationship between mental well-being and preparedness is bidirectional. On one hand, mental well-being contributes to a person's ability to be prepared. On the other hand, being prepared can enhance mental well-being. This synergy can be understood through several key mechanisms.

1. Emotional Resilience and Stress Management

Emotional resilience is the ability to adapt to stressful situations and bounce back from adversity. Preparedness fosters emotional resilience by equipping individuals with strategies and resources to manage stress. For example, having a well-thought-out emergency plan can reduce anxiety during crises, as individuals feel more in control and less overwhelmed.

Conversely, individuals with high emotional resilience are better equipped to prepare for various scenarios. They can remain calm and collected, think clearly, and make effective decisions under pressure. This ability to handle stress positively influences their overall mental well-being, creating a virtuous cycle of preparedness and resilience.

2. Cognitive Flexibility and Problem-Solving

Cognitive flexibility refers to the mental ability to switch between thinking about different concepts and to think about multiple concepts simultaneously. This skill is crucial for effective problem-solving and adaptability, which are essential components of preparedness.

Preparedness activities, such as planning and training, enhance cognitive flexibility by exposing individuals to a variety of scenarios and encouraging them to think creatively about solutions. For instance, regular practice of emergency drills helps individuals become more adept at handling unexpected situations, improving their ability to adapt quickly and effectively.

Moreover, individuals with strong cognitive flexibility are more likely to engage in preparedness activities, as they can envision different potential outcomes and plan accordingly. This proactive approach to problem-solving contributes to their mental well-being by reducing uncertainty and enhancing their sense of control over their environment.

3. Social Support and Community Preparedness

Social well-being is significantly influenced by the quality of one's relationships and social support network. Community preparedness initiatives, such as neighborhood watch programs or local disaster response teams, foster social connections and collaboration. These activities provide individuals with a sense of belonging and mutual support, which are critical for mental well-being.

Participating in community preparedness efforts not only enhances collective resilience but also strengthens individual mental health. The support and camaraderie found in these groups can alleviate feelings of isolation and anxiety, promoting a positive outlook and emotional stability.

4. Physical Health and Holistic Preparedness

Physical health is a foundational aspect of overall well-being and preparedness. Maintaining good physical health through regular exercise, a balanced diet, and adequate sleep enhances an individual's capacity to handle stress and recover from physical and mental challenges.

Physical preparedness, such as having a first aid kit and knowing basic emergency procedures, directly impacts mental well-being by providing a sense of security and readiness. Additionally, engaging in physical preparedness activities, like first aid training, can boost self-confidence and a sense of efficacy, further contributing to mental well-being.

Practical Strategies to Enhance Preparedness and Mental Well-Being

Understanding the connection between mental well-being and preparedness is essential, but practical application is equally important. Here are some strategies to enhance both:

1. Develop a Personal Preparedness Plan

Creating a comprehensive personal preparedness plan can significantly reduce anxiety and improve mental well-being. This plan should include:

Emergency contacts and communication strategies.

A list of essential supplies, such as food, water, and medications.

Evacuation routes and safe locations.

Procedures for various scenarios, including natural disasters and medical emergencies.

Having a well-structured plan ensures that individuals feel more secure and capable of handling unexpected situations.

2. Practice Mindfulness and Stress-Reduction Techniques

Incorporating mindfulness practices and stress-reduction techniques into daily routines can enhance emotional resilience and preparedness. Techniques such as meditation, deep breathing exercises, and yoga help individuals manage stress, maintain focus, and stay calm under pressure.

3. Engage in Regular Physical Activity

Regular physical activity is crucial for maintaining physical health and supporting mental well-being. Exercise releases endorphins, which improve mood and reduce stress. Activities such as jogging, swimming, or even walking can enhance physical preparedness and overall resilience.

4. Foster Strong Social Connections

Building and maintaining strong social connections is vital for mental well-being and preparedness. Engaging in community activities, joining support groups, and nurturing relationships with family and friends provide a robust support network.

These connections offer emotional support during challenging times and collaborative strength during crises.

5. *Continuously Learn and Adapt*

Embracing a mindset of continuous learning and adaptability is key to both preparedness and mental well-being. Attending workshops, participating in training sessions, and staying informed about potential risks and safety measures ensure individuals are always prepared for new challenges. This proactive approach fosters a sense of competence and confidence.

Case study

The Impact of Preparedness on Mental Well-Being

To further illustrate the connection between mental well-being and preparedness, let's examine a few case studies.

Case Study 1:

Community Response to Natural Disasters

In areas prone to natural disasters, such as hurricanes or earthquakes, communities that have established preparedness plans tend to experience lower levels of anxiety and psychological distress. For instance, a study conducted in coastal regions of the United States found that communities with robust disaster preparedness programs reported higher levels of mental well-being among residents. These programs included regular drills, clear communication channels, and readily available resources, which helped individuals feel more secure and supported during emergencies.

Case Study 2:

Individual Preparedness in Healthcare Settings

Healthcare workers, particularly those in high-stress environments such as emergency rooms, benefit greatly from preparedness training. Programs that focus on crisis management, psychological first aid, and stress reduction techniques have shown to improve the mental well-being of healthcare professionals. For example, a hospital in New York implemented a comprehensive preparedness program that included regular simulation exercises and resilience training. The program resulted in decreased burnout rates and improved job satisfaction among staff, demonstrating the positive impact of preparedness on mental well-being.

Case Study 3:

School-Based Preparedness Programs

Schools that incorporate preparedness programs into their curricula not only enhance the safety of students but also support their mental well-being. Programs that teach students how to respond to emergencies, manage stress, and support their peers foster a sense of empowerment and resilience. A school district in California introduced a preparedness curriculum that included mental health education, emergency response training, and peer support initiatives. The program led to increased student confidence, reduced anxiety, and a more supportive school environment.

The deep connection between mental well-being and preparedness underscores the importance of adopting a holistic approach to health and resilience. Preparedness, encompassing emotional, cognitive, social, and physical dimensions, plays a crucial role in enhancing mental well-being. By fostering emotional resilience, cognitive flexibility, social support, and physical health, preparedness equips individuals to navigate life's challenges with confidence and stability.

Implementing practical strategies, such as developing personal preparedness plans, practicing mindfulness, engaging in physical activity, fostering social connections, and embracing continuous learning, can significantly improve both preparedness and mental well-being. The positive outcomes observed in various case studies further validate the profound impact of preparedness on mental health.

Ultimately, investing in preparedness is an investment in mental well-being, enabling individuals and communities to thrive in the face of adversity. By recognizing and nurturing this connection, we can build a more resilient and mentally healthy society.

Chapter 8: Executing with Confidence

Harnessing the Confidence from Thorough Preparation

Confidence is an elusive yet essential component of success in various aspects of life, from personal achievements to professional endeavors. While some may attribute confidence to inherent personality traits or natural talent, a significant portion of it is derived from meticulous preparation. The relationship between preparation and confidence is profound and multifaceted, influencing not just outcomes but also personal growth and resilience.

Understanding Confidence and Its Importance

Confidence can be defined as a belief in one's abilities to accomplish a task or navigate a situation successfully. It is a crucial psychological trait that impacts motivation, performance, and resilience. Confident individuals are more likely to take on challenges, persevere through difficulties, and recover from setbacks. They tend to exhibit better decision-making skills, higher levels of creativity, and more effective communication.

However, confidence is not a static trait; it fluctuates based on experiences and perceptions of competence. Therefore, building and maintaining confidence is an ongoing process that often hinges on preparation.

The Psychology of Preparation

Preparation involves the systematic planning and practice necessary to achieve proficiency in a specific area. From a psychological perspective, preparation enhances confidence through several mechanisms:

Mastery and Competence: The more one practices and prepares, the more skilled they become. Mastery of skills leads to a sense of competence, which directly boosts confidence. This aligns with Albert Bandura's theory of self-efficacy, which posits that belief in one's ability to succeed in specific situations is built through mastery experiences.

Reducing Uncertainty: Preparation helps to anticipate and mitigate potential challenges, reducing the uncertainty that often undermines confidence. When individuals feel prepared, they are less likely to be thrown off by unexpected obstacles, which contributes to a steadier, more assured demeanor.

Cognitive Rehearsal: Engaging in mental practice and visualization is a form of preparation that strengthens neural pathways associated with performance. This technique not only improves actual skills but also enhances mental readiness, making individuals more confident in their abilities.

Emotional Regulation: Preparation can include strategies to manage stress and anxiety. Familiarity with the task at hand and having a clear action plan can reduce performance anxiety, allowing individuals to maintain composure and confidence even under pressure.

Practical Strategies for Effective Preparation

Harnessing confidence through preparation involves adopting practical strategies that can be tailored to various contexts, whether academic, professional, or personal.

Setting Clear Goals: Effective preparation begins with defining clear, achievable goals. Goals provide direction and purpose, helping to focus efforts and measure progress. They should be specific, measurable, attainable, relevant, and time-bound (SMART).

Developing a Plan: Once goals are set, developing a detailed plan is essential. This plan should outline the steps needed to achieve the goals, including resources, timelines, and potential obstacles. A well-structured plan acts as a roadmap, guiding efforts and ensuring comprehensive preparation.

Practice and Repetition: Repeated practice is fundamental to mastering any skill. Deliberate practice, which involves focused and structured repetition with the goal of continuous improvement, is particularly effective. This method emphasizes quality over quantity, encouraging individuals to refine their techniques and learn from mistakes.

Seeking Feedback: Constructive feedback is invaluable for effective preparation. It provides insights into areas of improvement and reinforces strengths. Seeking feedback from mentors, peers, or experts can accelerate the learning process and boost confidence.

Simulating Real Conditions: Practicing under conditions that closely mimic the actual performance environment can significantly enhance confidence. This includes simulations, mock exams, role-playing, or trial runs. Familiarity with the real conditions reduces anxiety and builds a sense of readiness.

Reflecting and Adjusting: Reflection is a critical component of preparation. Regularly assessing progress and adjusting the plan as needed ensures continuous improvement. Reflective practices help identify what works, what doesn't, and why, allowing for more effective and efficient preparation.

Case Studies and Examples

To illustrate the impact of thorough preparation on confidence, consider the following real-world examples:

Example 1: Athletes

Elite athletes often exemplify the power of preparation in building confidence. Olympic gymnast Simone Biles, for instance, undergoes rigorous training routines that involve not just physical practice but also mental conditioning. Her confidence in competition is a direct result of countless hours of preparation, including perfecting techniques, simulating competition scenarios, and employing visualization strategies.

Biles' preparation allows her to approach performances with a strong sense of confidence, knowing that she has honed her skills to the highest level. This confidence not only enhances her performance but also enables her to handle the immense pressure of competing on the world stage.

Example 2: Public Speaking

Public speaking is an area where preparation can dramatically influence confidence. Consider the experience of a corporate executive preparing for a critical presentation. Through thorough preparation—researching the topic, understanding the audience, rehearsing the speech, and anticipating questions—the executive can approach the presentation with confidence.

Effective public speakers often practice their delivery multiple times, receive feedback from peers, and refine their content and delivery based on this feedback. Such preparation minimizes the fear of forgetting key points or being unable to answer questions, thereby boosting confidence and improving the overall impact of the presentation.

Example 3: Academic Success

Students preparing for major exams also benefit significantly from thorough preparation. For instance, a medical student studying for the United States Medical Licensing Examination (USMLE) might follow a structured study plan over several months, incorporating practice tests, review sessions, and group studies.

This systematic preparation helps the student build a comprehensive understanding of the material and develop test-taking strategies. As a result, the student approaches the exam with confidence, knowing they are well-prepared to tackle the questions and manage their time effectively.

The Role of Resilience and Adaptability

While preparation is crucial for building confidence, it is also important to recognize the role of resilience and adaptability. Despite thorough preparation, unexpected challenges can still arise. In such cases, confidence also depends on one's ability to adapt and remain resilient.

Resilience: Resilience is the ability to bounce back from setbacks and maintain a positive outlook. Prepared individuals are often more resilient because they have developed a strong foundation of skills and knowledge that they can rely on. This foundation provides a buffer against the impact of failure or unforeseen difficulties.

Adaptability: Adaptability is the capacity to adjust one's approach in response to changing circumstances. Thorough preparation equips individuals with a deeper understanding of their domain, enabling them to adapt more effectively. For instance, a well-prepared entrepreneur facing market changes can pivot their business strategy based on their extensive preparation and knowledge of the industry.

The link between thorough preparation and confidence is clear and compelling. Preparation enhances skills, reduces uncertainty, improves mental readiness, and fosters emotional regulation, all of which contribute to a confident mindset. By setting clear goals, developing structured plans, engaging in deliberate practice, seeking feedback, simulating real conditions, and reflecting on progress, individuals can harness the transformative power of preparation to build and maintain confidence.

Whether in sports, public speaking, academic pursuits, or professional endeavors, the benefits of thorough preparation are evident. Prepared individuals not only perform better but also approach challenges with a sense of assurance and resilience that sets them apart. Ultimately, confidence born of thorough preparation is a reliable companion on the path to success, empowering individuals to achieve their fullest potential and navigate life's uncertainties with poise and determination.

Self-Doubt and Imposter Syndrome: *Their Dangers During the Preparation Stage*

Self-doubt and imposter syndrome are pervasive issues that many individuals face, particularly during periods of preparation for significant tasks or roles. These psychological phenomena can severely impact one's confidence, performance, and overall mental well-being.

Understanding Self-Doubt and Imposter Syndrome

Self-doubt refers to the lack of confidence in oneself and one's abilities. It manifests as persistent feelings of inadequacy, regardless of evidence to the contrary. Imposter syndrome, a related but distinct concept, is the internal experience of believing that one is not as competent as others perceive them to be. People with imposter syndrome often attribute their success to luck rather than their own skills and fear being exposed as a "fraud."

The Impact of Self-Doubt and Imposter Syndrome

Mental Health

Self-doubt and imposter syndrome can lead to chronic stress, anxiety, and depression. The constant fear of failure or being "found out" as a fraud creates a significant mental burden. For example, a student preparing for final exams might constantly second-guess their understanding of the material, leading to sleepless nights and heightened anxiety.

Performance

The impact on performance can be profound. Self-doubt can cause individuals to underperform due to a lack of confidence, while imposter syndrome may lead them to overwork themselves to prove their worth. A classic example is a young professional starting a new job who, despite their qualifications, feels they do not deserve their position and thus overcompensates by working excessively long hours.

Career Progression

Long-term career development can be hindered as well. Individuals may avoid applying for promotions or new opportunities because they believe they are not qualified, thus limiting their professional growth. For instance, an engineer might refrain from applying for a leadership position because they doubt their managerial capabilities, despite having the requisite experience and skills.

Examples from Different Fields

Academia

In academia, self-doubt and imposter syndrome are rampant, particularly among graduate students and early-career researchers. A PhD candidate might struggle with the belief that their research is not groundbreaking enough or that their knowledge is insufficient. This can lead to procrastination and difficulty in completing their dissertation.

Healthcare

Healthcare professionals, especially those in training, often experience these feelings. A medical resident might question their diagnostic skills, fearing that any mistake could have serious consequences. This doubt can result in excessive caution, slowing down decision-making processes and potentially affecting patient care.

Creative Arts

Artists, writers, and performers frequently battle imposter syndrome. A writer may feel that their latest novel does not measure up to their previous works or the works of their peers, leading to severe writer's block. Similarly, an actor might believe their recent success is a fluke and fear they will not be able to replicate it in future performances.

Case Studies

Sheryl Sandberg

Sheryl Sandberg, the COO of Facebook, has publicly spoken about her struggles with imposter syndrome. Despite her considerable achievements, she often felt that she was not truly qualified for her roles. This feeling persisted even as she climbed the corporate ladder, demonstrating that imposter syndrome can affect even the most successful individuals.

Neil Gaiman

Renowned author Neil Gaiman has also shared his experiences with imposter syndrome. Despite his numerous bestsellers and accolades, he frequently feels like a fraud and worries about being exposed as not truly talented. This illustrates how widespread and persistent these feelings can be, regardless of external success.

Strategies to Overcome Self-Doubt and Imposter Syndrome

Cognitive Behavioral Techniques

Cognitive Behavioral Therapy (CBT) techniques can be very effective in addressing self-doubt and imposter syndrome. These techniques involve identifying and challenging negative thought patterns and replacing them with more constructive ones. For example, individuals can keep a journal to track their accomplishments and the positive feedback they receive, which can help counteract feelings of inadequacy.

Mentorship and Support Networks

Having a mentor or a supportive peer group can make a significant difference. Mentors can provide reassurance and constructive feedback, helping individuals to see their true value. Support groups allow people to share their experiences and realize that they are not alone in their feelings, which can be incredibly validating.

Mindfulness and Self-Compassion

Practicing mindfulness and self-compassion can help individuals manage their self-doubt. Mindfulness involves staying present and non-judgmental about one's thoughts and feelings, while self-compassion involves treating oneself with kindness and understanding. These practices can reduce the intensity of negative self-perceptions.

Skill Development

Continuing to develop skills and knowledge can boost confidence. Engaging in professional development or seeking additional training can help individuals feel more competent and secure in their abilities. For example, attending workshops or pursuing further education can provide tangible proof of one's expertise.

Setting Realistic Goals

Setting realistic and achievable goals can help mitigate feelings of inadequacy. Breaking larger tasks into smaller, manageable steps can make the process seem less daunting and provide a sense of accomplishment as each step is completed. This approach can be particularly helpful in academic and professional settings.

Self-doubt and imposter syndrome are significant psychological barriers that can severely impact an individual's performance, mental health, and career progression. These phenomena are prevalent across various fields, affecting students, professionals, and creatives alike. Through understanding and addressing these issues with appropriate strategies, individuals can overcome these challenges and realize their full potential. The key lies in recognizing these feelings as common and manageable, rather than insurmountable obstacles.

Maintaining composure and adaptability

Maintaining composure and adaptability in high-pressure situations is a critical skill in both personal and professional settings. This ability not only enhances decision-making and performance but also contributes to overall well-being and resilience. Here, we will explore various strategies to cultivate and maintain these attributes, drawing on psychological principles, practical techniques, and illustrative examples.

Understanding Composure and Adaptability

Composure refers to the state of being calm and in control of oneself. It involves managing emotions, maintaining a clear mind, and behaving rationally under stress.

Adaptability is the ability to adjust to new conditions or changes in the environment. It requires flexibility in thinking and behavior, as well as the capacity to learn and apply new skills quickly.

Psychological Foundations

1. Stress Response and Management:

Fight-or-Flight Response: High-pressure situations often trigger this response, releasing adrenaline and cortisol. While useful in short bursts, prolonged activation can be detrimental.

Mindfulness and Relaxation Techniques: Practices such as deep breathing, meditation, and progressive muscle relaxation help activate the parasympathetic nervous system, promoting calmness.

2. Cognitive Reappraisal:

Reframing: Changing the way one perceives a situation can significantly alter its emotional impact. Viewing challenges as opportunities for growth rather than threats can reduce stress.

Positive Visualization: Imagining successful outcomes can enhance confidence and composure.

3. Emotional Intelligence:

Self-Awareness: Recognizing one's emotional triggers and responses is the first step toward managing them.

Self-Regulation: Developing the ability to control impulsive reactions and think before acting.

Practical Techniques

1. Preparation and Planning:

Scenario Planning: Anticipate possible challenges and devise strategies to address them. This reduces uncertainty and increases confidence.

Skill Development: Regular practice and skill enhancement prepare individuals to handle unexpected situations more effectively.

2. Time Management:

Prioritization: Focus on high-impact tasks and allocate time efficiently to avoid last-minute stress.

Breaks and Rest: Regular breaks prevent burnout and maintain cognitive function.

3. Communication:

Clear and Concise: Effective communication reduces misunderstandings and aligns team efforts.

Active Listening: Understanding others' perspectives can provide new insights and solutions.

Illustrative Examples

1. Healthcare:

Scenario: An emergency room doctor faces multiple critical patients simultaneously.

Strategies: By staying composed through deep breathing exercises and relying on practiced protocols, the doctor prioritizes tasks and delegates effectively, ensuring each patient receives timely care.

2. Business:

Scenario: A project manager must present a critical report to stakeholders amid unforeseen technical issues.

Strategies: The manager remains calm by using cognitive reappraisal, viewing the situation as a chance to demonstrate problem-solving skills. By clearly communicating the issues and potential solutions, the manager maintains stakeholder confidence.

3. Sports:

Scenario: A basketball player faces a high-pressure free throw in the final seconds of a game.

Strategies: Utilizing positive visualization and controlled breathing, the player focuses on the mechanics of the shot rather than the pressure, increasing the likelihood of success.

Long-Term Strategies

1. Building Resilience:

Regular Physical Exercise: Enhances overall stress tolerance and mental clarity.

Healthy Lifestyle Choices: Balanced nutrition, sufficient sleep, and hydration support optimal brain function.

2. Continuous Learning:

Professional Development: Engaging in continuous education and training keeps skills sharp and adaptable.

Feedback Mechanisms: Actively seeking and incorporating feedback improves performance and adaptability.

3. Support Systems:

Mentorship: Guidance from experienced individuals provides perspective and advice in high-pressure situations.

Peer Support: Collaborative environments foster shared problem-solving and emotional support.

Maintaining composure and adaptability in high-pressure situations is a multifaceted skill that can be developed through psychological understanding, practical techniques, and consistent practice. By preparing effectively, managing stress responses, and cultivating emotional intelligence, individuals can navigate challenging circumstances with confidence and resilience. Whether in healthcare, business, sports, or everyday life, these strategies enable individuals to perform at their best and thrive under pressure.

Chapter 9: Reflecting and Learning

Reflection and self-assessment are crucial components of the learning process, offering numerous benefits that can enhance personal and professional development. These practices allow individuals to critically evaluate their experiences, identify strengths and weaknesses, and set goals for future growth. In this exploration, we will delve into the significance of reflection and self-assessment through various illustrative stories and detailed explanations.

The Importance of Reflection and Self-Assessment

The Concept of Reflection

Reflection is the process of looking back on one's actions, experiences, and outcomes to gain deeper understanding and insights. This introspective practice enables individuals to consider what they did well, what they could improve, and how their actions align with their goals and values.

The Concept of Self-Assessment

Self-assessment involves evaluating one's performance, skills, and knowledge. It requires honest and objective analysis, often leading to the identification of areas for improvement and the recognition of achievements. Self-assessment helps individuals take responsibility for their learning and development.

The Student's Journey

Setting the Scene

Emily, a university student, has just completed a challenging semester. She took a variety of courses, each demanding in different ways. As the semester ends, Emily feels a mix of relief and uncertainty about her performance.

Reflection in Action

Emily decides to spend a weekend reflecting on her semester. She revisits her notes, assignments, and exam results. She remembers the late nights studying, the group projects, and the feedback from her professors. By doing this, Emily identifies her strengths, such as her strong analytical skills and ability to work well in groups. She also recognizes her weaknesses, particularly her tendency to procrastinate and her struggles with time management.

Self-Assessment Outcomes

Armed with this information, Emily conducts a self-assessment. She rates her performance in each course and compares it to her initial expectations. She realizes that while she excelled in her favorite subjects, she neglected the ones she found less interesting. Emily sets specific goals for the next semester: to improve her time management, seek help in challenging subjects, and maintain her strong performance in areas she enjoys.

The Professional's Reflection

A New Project

John, a project manager at a tech company, has just completed a major project. The project was complex, involving multiple teams and tight deadlines. Despite the challenges, the project was delivered on time and received positive feedback from the client.

Reflecting on the Experience

John takes time to reflect on the project. He gathers feedback from his team, reviews project documents, and considers the obstacles they faced. Through reflection, John acknowledges the effective communication and collaboration that contributed to the project's success. However, he also notes areas for improvement, such as the need for better risk management and more accurate time estimations.

Implementing Self-Assessment

John conducts a self-assessment, evaluating his leadership skills and project management techniques. He identifies his strengths, such as his ability to motivate his team and his problem-solving skills. He also recognizes the need to improve his planning processes. John sets goals to attend a risk management workshop and to develop a more detailed project planning template for future projects.

The Athlete's Evaluation

Post-Competition Analysis

Sara, a competitive swimmer, has just finished a major swim meet. She achieved personal best times in some events but fell short in others. After the competition, Sara feels a mix of satisfaction and disappointment.

Reflecting on Performance

Sara spends time reflecting on her performance. She watches videos of her races, reviews her training logs, and talks to her coach. Through this reflection, Sara identifies the factors that contributed to her successes, such as her consistent training and strong mental focus. She also notes the areas where she struggled, like her technique in the backstroke event and her endurance in longer races.

Self-Assessment and Future Goals

Sara conducts a self-assessment, comparing her current performance to her goals. She acknowledges her achievements and sets new targets for the upcoming season. Sara decides to focus on improving her backstroke technique and enhancing her endurance. She creates a detailed training plan with her coach, incorporating these goals to ensure continuous improvement.

Benefits of Reflection and Self-Assessment

Enhancing Self-Awareness

Reflection and self-assessment enhance self-awareness by encouraging individuals to take an honest look at their actions and outcomes. This increased self-awareness helps people understand their strengths and weaknesses, leading to more effective personal and professional development.

Promoting Continuous Improvement

By regularly reflecting and assessing their performance, individuals can identify areas for improvement and set specific goals. This promotes a mindset of continuous improvement, fostering growth and development over time.

Building Confidence and Motivation

Recognizing one's achievements through reflection and self-assessment can boost confidence and motivation. When individuals see the progress they have made, they are more likely to stay motivated and committed to their goals.

Encouraging Responsibility and Accountability

Self-assessment encourages individuals to take responsibility for their learning and development. By evaluating their performance and setting goals, they become more accountable for their actions and outcomes.

Practical Steps for Effective Reflection and Self-Assessment

Establish a Regular Practice

To make reflection and self-assessment effective, it is important to establish a regular practice. Set aside dedicated time after completing significant tasks or projects to reflect and assess your performance.

Use Structured Tools and Frameworks

Using structured tools and frameworks can help guide the reflection and self-assessment process. Journals, checklists, and feedback forms can provide a systematic approach to evaluating experiences and identifying areas for improvement.

Seek Feedback from Others

Incorporating feedback from others can provide valuable insights and perspectives. Seek input from peers, mentors, or supervisors to gain a more comprehensive understanding of your performance.

Set Specific and Achievable Goals

Based on your reflection and self-assessment, set specific and achievable goals for future improvement. Make sure these goals are clear, measurable, and aligned with your overall objectives.

Reflection and self-assessment are powerful tools for personal and professional development. By regularly engaging in these practices, individuals can gain deeper insights into their actions, identify areas for improvement, and set goals for continuous growth. Through the stories of Emily, John, and Sara, we see how reflection and self-assessment can lead to enhanced self-awareness, improved performance, and greater motivation. Embracing these practices can help individuals take control of their learning and development, ultimately leading to greater success and fulfillment in their endeavors.

Identifying strengths

Identifying strengths during the preparation stage of any endeavor, whether it be personal development, business planning, team formation, or project management, is crucial for several reasons. By understanding and leveraging strengths, individuals and organizations can optimize their performance, build confidence, and create a solid foundation for success.

1. Enhancing Self-Awareness and Confidence

Knowing one's strengths helps in building self-awareness, which is fundamental for personal growth. When individuals recognize what they are good at, they gain confidence in their abilities. This confidence propels them to take on challenges and strive for excellence.

Example:

Consider a student preparing for competitive exams. If the student knows that their strength lies in mathematics, they can allocate more time to subjects they find challenging while using their proficiency in mathematics to score high in that section. This strategic preparation can lead to overall better performance in the exams.

2. Optimizing Resource Allocation

In project management, identifying the strengths of team members ensures that tasks are assigned to those best suited to complete them efficiently. This optimizes resource allocation and enhances productivity.

Example:

In a software development project, if a team member excels in coding but struggles with design, assigning them to the coding tasks while giving the design work to a team member who has a knack for creativity will yield better results. This not only boosts the morale of the individuals but also leads to higher quality outputs.

3. Strategic Planning and Competitive Advantage

Businesses that understand their core strengths can develop strategies that leverage these strengths to gain a competitive advantage. This could mean focusing on areas where the company excels and differentiating from competitors.

Example:

A tech company known for its innovative software solutions might focus on developing cutting-edge applications rather than venturing into hardware where it lacks expertise. This strategic focus allows the company to maintain a competitive edge in its niche.

4. Fostering Collaboration and Team Dynamics

In team settings, identifying and acknowledging each member's strengths fosters a culture of respect and collaboration. Team members are more likely to trust each other's capabilities, leading to better teamwork and higher performance.

Example:

In a marketing team, one member might be excellent at data analysis while another excels at creative content creation. Recognizing these strengths allows the team to collaborate effectively, with each member contributing their best to achieve common goals.

5. *Driving Innovation and Problem-Solving*

Strength-based approaches encourage individuals to use their innate talents and skills to drive innovation. When people work within their areas of strength, they are more likely to think creatively and come up with effective solutions to problems.

Example:

In a research and development department, a scientist with a strength in theoretical modeling might pair with an experimentalist who excels in lab work. Together, they can innovate more effectively than if each were working outside their comfort zones.

6. *Building Resilience and Adaptability*

Identifying strengths can also help in building resilience. When individuals and organizations are aware of their strengths, they can better navigate through challenges and adapt to changes by relying on these strengths.

Example:

A company that identifies its strength in customer service can rely on this capability to maintain customer loyalty during economic downturns, even if it faces challenges in other areas like supply chain disruptions.

7. Improving Motivation and Job Satisfaction

When people work in roles that align with their strengths, they are generally more motivated and satisfied with their work. This leads to higher levels of engagement and productivity.

Example:

An employee who is naturally good at interpersonal communication might find great satisfaction in a customer-facing role, leading to higher job satisfaction and lower turnover rates.

Identifying strengths in the preparation stage is a critical step in achieving success in any domain. It enhances self-awareness, optimizes resource allocation, supports strategic planning, fosters collaboration, drives innovation, builds resilience, and improves motivation and job satisfaction. By recognizing and leveraging strengths, individuals and organizations can create a strong foundation for reaching their goals and achieving sustained success.

How can you Identifying the areas of improvement in the preparation stage?

Identifying areas of improvement in the preparation stage involves a thorough evaluation of current processes, practices, and outcomes.

Review Goals and Objectives:

Ensure that the preparation stage goals are clear, specific, and aligned with the overall project objectives.

Evaluate whether the current processes are designed to meet these goals effectively.

Gather Feedback:

Collect feedback from team members involved in the preparation stage.

Use surveys, interviews, or focus groups to understand their perspectives on what is working well and what needs improvement.

Analyze Past Performance:

Review past projects or tasks to identify patterns of issues or delays.

Analyze key performance indicators (KPIs) and metrics to pinpoint areas where performance did not meet expectations.

Conduct a SWOT Analysis:

Identify Strengths, Weaknesses, Opportunities, and Threats related to the preparation stage.

Use this analysis to focus on weaknesses and threats that can be converted into areas of improvement.

Benchmarking:

Compare your processes with industry best practices or standards.

Identify gaps between your current practices and those recognized as effective within your industry.

Process Mapping:

Create detailed process maps of the preparation stage.

Look for bottlenecks, redundancies, or steps that do not add value.

Risk Assessment:

Identify potential risks and issues that could arise during the preparation stage.

Develop strategies to mitigate these risks, which can highlight areas that need strengthening.

Resource Utilization Review:

Evaluate the allocation and utilization of resources (time, personnel, equipment).

Identify any inefficiencies or areas where resources are under or over-utilized.

Stakeholder Input:

Engage with stakeholders to gather their insights and expectations.

Ensure their needs are being considered and addressed in the preparation stage.

Training and Skill Gaps:

Assess the skills and knowledge of the team involved in the preparation stage.

Identify any gaps and provide necessary training or resources to bridge them.

Technology and Tools Evaluation:

Review the technology and tools being used in the preparation stage.

Determine if they are the most effective options available or if there are better alternatives.

Continuous Improvement Programs:

Implement programs that encourage continuous feedback and incremental improvements.

Regularly review and update processes based on new insights and feedback.

By systematically analyzing these areas, you can identify specific points that need enhancement and develop targeted strategies to improve the preparation stage effectively.

Chapter 10: The Journey Continues

Title: *The Endless Journey of Preparation*

The Seeds of Ambition

On the outskirts of a bustling city, nestled among rolling hills and verdant fields, lay the quiet town of Willowbrook. It was here that young Elena Fisher grew up, nurtured by the rhythms of a close-knit community and the enduring support of her family. From a young age, Elena was curious and driven, always dreaming of achieving something extraordinary.

Elena's father, Thomas, was a master carpenter, revered for his meticulous craftsmanship. He often told her, "Success doesn't happen overnight, Elena. It's the result of relentless preparation and hard work." These words, simple yet profound, resonated deeply with her, planting the seeds of ambition.

The First Steps

In high school, Elena's ambition manifested in her passion for science. She devoured textbooks, spent countless hours in the lab, and entered every science fair she could. Her diligence paid off when she won a prestigious regional science competition. The accolade bolstered her confidence, but her father's words kept her grounded.

Thomas encouraged her to view this victory not as an endpoint, but as a milestone. "Preparation, Elena, is a lifelong practice," he reminded her. "It's about continually improving, learning, and growing."

Inspired by his wisdom, Elena applied to one of the best universities in the country, aiming to study biochemistry. Her acceptance letter arrived in the spring of her senior year, and with it came a profound realization: the real journey was just beginning.

The University Challenge

University life was a whirlwind of lectures, lab work, and late-night study sessions. Elena quickly realized that her high school efforts, while commendable, were just the foundation. The academic rigor required an even greater level of preparation. She faced numerous challenges, from complex experiments that failed to daunting exams that tested her resolve.

Yet, Elena embraced these challenges with unwavering determination. She joined study groups, sought help from professors, and constantly refined her study techniques. Each setback became an opportunity to learn, to prepare better for the next hurdle. The more she delved into her studies, the more she recognized the truth in her father's advice: preparation was indeed a lifelong journey.

Her hard work culminated in a groundbreaking research project on gene therapy, which garnered attention from several prestigious institutions. Upon graduation, she received multiple offers for PhD programs. She chose a renowned university that specialized in genetic research, eager to push the boundaries of her knowledge further.

The Professional Realm

The transition from academia to the professional world was another leap into the unknown. As a young scientist in a leading biotech company, Elena found herself among brilliant minds, each contributing to cutting-edge advancements. The stakes were higher, the competition fiercer, and the margin for error slimmer.

In her new role, preparation took on new dimensions. It wasn't just about knowledge and skills; it was also about staying abreast of the latest research, understanding market trends, and honing her communication abilities. She learned to navigate the corporate landscape, where collaboration and leadership were as crucial as scientific acumen.

Elena's commitment to lifelong preparation distinguished her from her peers. She was often the first to arrive at the lab and the last to leave. Her thoroughness in planning experiments, coupled with her innovative thinking, led to significant breakthroughs. One such breakthrough was a novel method for delivering gene therapy, which had the potential to revolutionize treatments for genetic disorders.

Her achievements did not go unnoticed. She was promoted to lead a team of researchers, a role that required not only scientific expertise but also the ability to mentor and inspire others. Elena thrived in this role, always emphasizing the importance of preparation to her team.

The Personal Journey

Amidst her professional accomplishments, Elena did not neglect her personal growth. She took up running, initially as a way to clear her mind after long hours in the lab. Over time, it became a passion. She trained rigorously, setting new personal goals each year. The discipline and dedication required for running mirrored her approach to her career, reinforcing the notion that preparation was integral to all aspects of life.

Elena also pursued mindfulness and meditation, recognizing the importance of mental well-being in maintaining her high-performance levels. These practices helped her manage stress and maintain a balanced perspective, essential qualities in her demanding profession.

She invested time in relationships, understanding that a strong support network was crucial for sustained growth. Her friendships, built on mutual respect and shared experiences, provided solace and motivation. Her father, now retired, remained her steadfast advisor, their conversations a source of wisdom and encouragement.

The Ripple Effect

Elena's dedication to lifelong preparation began to influence those around her. Her team, inspired by her example, adopted a culture of continuous learning and improvement. They celebrated each other's successes and viewed failures as opportunities for growth. This collaborative spirit led to several groundbreaking discoveries and solidified their position as leaders in the field.

Outside the lab, Elena volunteered as a mentor for aspiring young scientists, emphasizing the importance of preparation and perseverance. Her story resonated with many, and she became a sought-after speaker at conferences and seminars. She relished these opportunities to share her journey, hoping to inspire others to embrace preparation as a lifelong practice.

The Legacy of Preparation

Years passed, and Elena's contributions to science continued to grow. Her work in gene therapy transformed countless lives, and her leadership cultivated a generation of innovative thinkers. Despite her success, she remained grounded, always striving to learn and improve.

One day, while addressing a group of young researchers, she reflected on her journey. "Preparation isn't just about achieving success," she said. "It's about becoming the best version of yourself. It's about resilience, growth, and the relentless pursuit of excellence. It's a journey without a final destination, but one that enriches every step of the way."

As Elena looked out at the eager faces before her, she saw herself in them—full of dreams and potential. She realized that her greatest accomplishment was not the accolades or the breakthroughs, but the enduring impact of her philosophy on others.

Elena's journey was a testament to the power of preparation. It was a journey marked by challenges and triumphs, learning and growth. Her story was a reminder that preparation is not a finite task, but an ongoing process that shapes our lives and the world around us.

In the quiet moments, as she walked through the fields of Willowbrook or ran along familiar paths, Elena found peace in the realization that her father's wisdom had guided her well. She had embraced preparation as a lifelong practice, and in doing so, she had discovered the true essence of personal and professional growth.

And so, the journey continued—endlessly, beautifully, and with unwavering dedication.

Conclusion -

The Power of Preparation: Transforming Potential into Reality

In every story of success, there lies an undercurrent of preparation—a relentless, unseen force shaping the outcomes we admire. From the athlete training in the early hours before dawn to the artist honing their craft through countless iterations, preparation is the silent architect of achievement. While talent and luck play their roles, it is preparation that bridges the gap between potential and reality. This powerful principle can transform not only our professional endeavors but every facet of our lives. Let us explore how the principles of preparation can inspire us to create our own paths to success.

The Essence of Preparation

Preparation is not merely an act but a mindset. It embodies the belief that our future is not determined by chance but by the actions we take today. This mindset transforms challenges into opportunities and setbacks into stepping stones. It requires foresight, discipline, and an unwavering commitment to our goals.

When we prepare, we invest in ourselves. We acknowledge that excellence is not a destination but a journey. This journey demands dedication, sacrifice, and a willingness to embrace the process. By preparing, we build a foundation that allows us to weather the storms of uncertainty and seize the opportunities that come our way.

The Benefits of Preparation

1. Building Confidence: Preparation instills confidence. When we are well-prepared, we approach challenges with a sense of assurance. We know our strengths and have addressed our weaknesses. This self-awareness empowers us to take bold steps and make decisive choices.

2. Enhancing Performance: Consistent preparation sharpens our skills and enhances our performance. Whether it's rehearsing for a presentation, practicing a musical piece, or training for a marathon, the time we invest in preparation translates into improved performance. It allows us to perform at our best when it matters most.

3. Reducing Stress: Uncertainty often breeds stress. Preparation mitigates this by providing a clear plan and a sense of control. When we know we have done everything possible to prepare, we can approach situations with a calm and focused mind.

4. Seizing Opportunities: Opportunities rarely come with warning. Preparation positions us to recognize and seize these moments. It ensures we are ready when the right opportunity presents itself, enabling us to act swiftly and effectively.

5. Fostering Resilience: Life is unpredictable, and setbacks are inevitable. Preparation fosters resilience by equipping us with the tools and strategies to navigate challenges. It teaches us to adapt, learn from our experiences, and emerge stronger.

Applying the Principles of Preparation

To harness the power of preparation, we must integrate its principles into our daily lives. Here are some practical steps to get started:

1. Set Clear Goals

Preparation begins with a clear vision. Identify what you want to achieve and set specific, measurable, attainable, relevant, and time-bound (SMART) goals. This clarity will guide your preparation efforts and keep you focused on what truly matters.

2. Create a Plan

Once you have defined your goals, create a detailed plan. Break down your goals into smaller, manageable tasks and set deadlines for each. This plan will serve as a roadmap, guiding your actions and ensuring you stay on track.

3. Invest in Learning

Knowledge is a key component of preparation. Continuously seek to expand your knowledge and skills. Read books, take courses, attend workshops, and learn from others who have achieved what you aspire to. The more you know, the better equipped you will be to navigate challenges and capitalize on opportunities.

4. Practice Diligently

Practice is the cornerstone of preparation. Dedicate time each day to practice and refine your skills. Embrace the repetition and perseverance required to master your craft. Remember, excellence is achieved through consistent effort and practice.

5. Embrace Failure

Failure is an inevitable part of any journey. Instead of fearing it, embrace it as a learning opportunity. Analyze your mistakes, learn from them, and adjust your approach. Each failure brings you one step closer to success.

6. Stay Organized

Organization is crucial for effective preparation. Keep your workspace tidy, manage your time efficiently, and prioritize your tasks. Use tools like calendars, to-do lists, and project management software to stay organized and focused.

7. Maintain Discipline

Discipline is the backbone of preparation. Stay committed to your goals and follow through on your plans, even when it gets tough. Cultivate habits that support your preparation efforts, such as regular exercise, healthy eating, and adequate rest.

8. Seek Support

Surround yourself with a supportive network of family, friends, mentors, and peers. Seek their advice, encouragement, and feedback. Their support will help you stay motivated and accountable on your journey.

The Ripple Effect of Preparation

The impact of preparation extends beyond individual success. It creates a ripple effect, inspiring and empowering others to pursue their own goals. When we lead by example and demonstrate the power of preparation, we contribute to a culture of excellence and resilience.

Consider the story of a young entrepreneur who meticulously prepares for every pitch. Her dedication and preparation not only secure funding for her business but also inspire her team to strive for excellence. Her story becomes a beacon of hope and motivation for aspiring entrepreneurs, showing them that success is within reach with the right preparation.

Similarly, a teacher who prepares engaging and impactful lessons creates a positive learning environment. Their preparation not only enhances their students' learning experience but also instills in them the value of hard work and preparation. These students carry these lessons into their future endeavors, creating a cycle of success and preparation.

Stories of Preparation and Success

Thomas Edison: One of the most famous inventors, Thomas Edison, once said, "Genius is one percent inspiration and ninety-nine percent perspiration." Edison's relentless preparation and experimentation led to the invention of the electric light bulb. He conducted over a thousand failed experiments before achieving success, demonstrating the importance of perseverance and preparation.

Serena Williams: Tennis champion Serena Williams is known for her rigorous training regimen and unwavering dedication to preparation. Her success on the court is a testament to the countless hours she has invested in practice and preparation. Williams' story inspires athletes and non-athletes alike to recognize the power of preparation in achieving excellence.

J.K. Rowling: Before becoming one of the best-selling authors of all time, J.K. Rowling faced numerous rejections for her Harry Potter manuscript. However, her meticulous preparation and belief in her story kept her going. Her journey from struggling writer to literary icon highlights the importance of preparation, perseverance, and believing in one's potential.

Conclusion: The Journey of Preparation

Preparation is a journey, not a destination. It is an ongoing process of learning, practicing, and refining. It requires patience, persistence, and a belief in the power of small, consistent efforts.

As we embark on our journeys, let us embrace the principles of preparation. Let us set clear goals, create detailed plans, and invest in continuous learning. Let us practice diligently, embrace failure, and maintain discipline. Let us seek support from those around us and stay organized in our efforts.

By integrating these principles into our lives, we unlock our potential and transform our dreams into reality. We become the architects of our future, building a foundation for success that withstands the test of time.

Remember, preparation is not just about achieving our goals; it is about becoming the best version of ourselves. It is about cultivating a mindset that embraces challenges, values hard work, and believes in the power of preparation. As we prepare, we inspire others to do the same, creating a ripple effect that transforms not only our lives but the world around us.

So, let us commit to the journey of preparation. Let us take the first step today and continue to move forward with purpose and determination. The road may be long and challenging, but with preparation as our guide, we can achieve greatness and make our mark on the world.

Prepare for achieving success

We stand at the precipice of a journey, a journey toward success. Each one of us carries within us the spark of potential, the seed of greatness waiting to be nurtured. The road ahead may be long and winding, filled with challenges and obstacles, but it is in these moments of preparation that we forge our path to triumph.

Success is not an accident; it is a deliberate, intentional process. It begins with a mindset, a commitment to excellence, and an unwavering belief in our abilities. It is in the quiet moments of preparation, when no one is watching, that we lay the foundation for our future victories.

Imagine a sculptor, chipping away at a block of marble. Each strike of the chisel, each moment of contemplation, brings them closer to their masterpiece. Similarly, our preparation is the chisel that shapes our destiny. It is the hours spent honing our skills, the dedication to learning and growing, and the resilience to keep moving forward, even when the going gets tough.

Success requires vision. We must see beyond the immediate challenges and visualize our goals with clarity and conviction. This vision will guide us, keeping us focused and motivated. It will remind us why we started, why we chose this path, and why we must persevere.

Preparation demands discipline. It requires us to show up every day, to put in the work, and to stay committed, even when it's difficult. Discipline is the bridge between our goals and our accomplishments. It is the silent partner in our journey, ensuring that we stay on course and continue to push ourselves to be better.

In this preparation time, embrace failure as a teacher. Each setback is an opportunity to learn, to grow, and to refine our approach. Success is not a straight line; it is a series of ebbs and flows, of highs and lows. It is our ability to rise after each fall, to learn from our mistakes, and to keep moving forward that defines our journey.

Surround yourself with positivity and support. The people we choose to associate with can lift us up or pull us down. Seek out those who inspire you, who challenge you to be better, and who believe in your potential. Together, we can achieve more than we ever could alone.

Finally, remember that success is a journey, not a destination. It is a continuous process of growth, learning, and improvement. Celebrate your milestones, but never become complacent. Always strive for more, for better, for greatness.

As we prepare for the challenges and opportunities ahead, let us embrace the journey with open hearts and determined minds. Let us commit to the hard work, the discipline, and the resilience required to achieve our dreams. Together, we can transform our potential into reality and achieve the success we so passionately seek.

Winning Performance

We live in a world that often celebrates the final product—the winning goal, the groundbreaking discovery, the award-winning performance. But what is frequently overlooked is the journey that leads to these moments of triumph. At the core of every success story, behind every achievement, lies the unseen, often unglamorous process of preparation.

Preparation is not merely about planning; it's about laying the groundwork for success, building a foundation that can support your ambitions, and transforming potential into reality. It is the countless hours of practice, the diligent research, the late nights, and early mornings spent honing your craft. It is the willingness to do what others are not willing to do, to invest in yourself, and to strive for excellence even when no one is watching.

Consider the athlete who trains tirelessly, day after day, year after year, for a chance to compete on the world stage. Their victory is not won in the moment of the race, but in the thousands of hours spent preparing. The same is true for the scientist who makes a groundbreaking discovery, the artist who creates a masterpiece, and the entrepreneur who builds a successful business. Their achievements are the culmination of relentless preparation.

Preparation is powerful because it equips us to seize opportunities when they arise. It allows us to approach challenges with confidence, knowing that we have done everything within our power to be ready. It transforms uncertainty into a calculated risk, and potential failure into a stepping stone for success.

So, how can we apply the principles of preparation in our own lives?

Set Clear Goals: Know what you are preparing for. Define your objectives and create a roadmap to achieve them. Clear goals give direction to your efforts and help you stay focused.

Invest in Learning: Continuously seek knowledge and skills that are relevant to your goals. Education and self-improvement are lifelong processes. Embrace them.

Practice Diligently: Dedicate time to practice and refine your skills. Repetition builds mastery. Don't shy away from the hard work required to excel.

Plan for Obstacles: Anticipate challenges and prepare for them. Have contingency plans in place. Being prepared for setbacks ensures they do not derail your progress.

Stay Consistent: Preparation is not a one-time effort; it is an ongoing commitment. Consistency is key. Make preparation a habit, and you will find that over time, small efforts compound into significant achievements.

Reflect and Adjust: Regularly review your progress and be willing to adjust your plans. Reflection helps you learn from your experiences and improve your strategies.

By embracing the principles of preparation, you are not only setting yourself up for success but also building resilience and confidence. When you prepare thoroughly, you can face challenges head-on, knowing that you have the skills and knowledge to overcome them.

Remember that every great achievement starts long before the moment of success. It starts with the quiet, determined effort to prepare. So, I encourage each of you to commit to preparation in your own lives. Set your goals, invest in your growth, practice with diligence, and be consistent. Your future self will thank you, and the world will witness the extraordinary results of your dedication.